ABOUT
FICTION

Books by Wright Morris

Novels
A LIFE
WAR GAMES
FIRE SERMON
IN ORBIT
ONE DAY
CAUSE FOR WONDER
WHAT A WAY TO GO
CEREMONY IN LONE TREE
LOVE AMONG THE CANNIBALS
THE FIELD OF VISION
THE HUGE SEASON
THE DEEP SLEEP
THE WORKS OF LOVE
MAN AND BOY
THE WORLD IN THE ATTIC
THE MAN WHO WAS THERE
MY UNCLE DUDLEY

Photo-Text
LOVE AFFAIR: A VENETIAN JOURNAL
GOD'S COUNTRY AND MY PEOPLE
THE HOME PLACE
THE INHABITANTS

Essays
ABOUT FICTION
A BILL OF RITES, A BILL OF WRONGS, A BILL OF GOODS
THE TERRITORY AHEAD

Anthology
WRIGHT MORRIS: A READER

ABOUT
FICTION

REVERENT REFLECTIONS
ON THE NATURE OF FICTION

WITH

IRREVERENT OBSERVATIONS
ON WRITERS, READERS,
& OTHER ABUSES

WRIGHT
MORRIS

HARPER & ROW, PUBLISHERS
New York, Evanston, San Francisco, London

For my students:

readers and writers

ABOUT FICTION. Copyright © 1975 by Wright Morris. All rights reserved. Printed in the United States of America. No part of this book may be used or reproduced in any manner whatsoever without written permission except in the case of brief quotations embodied in critical articles and reviews. For information address Harper & Row, Publishers, Inc., 10 East 53rd Street, New York, N.Y. 10022. Published simultaneously in Canada by Fitzhenry & Whiteside Limited, Toronto.

FIRST EDITION

Designed by Janice Stern

Library of Congress Cataloging in Publication Data

Morris, Wright, 1910–
    About fiction.
    1. Fiction—20th century—History and criticism
I. Title.
PN3503.M62   809.3′3   74–6771
ISBN 0–06–013082–2

CONTENTS

To the Reader

About Fiction *is a short book on an immense subject. Those larger pastures where the critic loves to dwell, the hills and dales of rhetoric, theme, and structure, preoccupy the writer as he writes but are of limited interest to the reader. Critics too love to write, and the fiction they write about fiction is called criticism. Most writers are appreciative of this attention, since they would rather be read and not liked than liked and not read.*

In this primer I write propaganda in the interests of good fiction. It's about everything, once we come to know what it's all about.

W. M.

Our own journey is entirely imaginative.
Therein lies its strength.

Céline

We are all here on earth to help each other,
but what the others are here for, God only
knows.

W. H. Auden

What Is Fiction?

We are a practical people, down to earth, fact-minded, ill at ease with abstractions and high-falutin' language, the all-American grain of our minds being one we either sand down or polish up. Although we attempt to face up to and live by the facts, we carry on the business of living in fiction. We do because we can't help it. Only fiction will accommodate the facts of life.

Before they made tools, perhaps before they made trouble, men and women were busy at the loom of fiction looking for clues to becoming more human. The proven facts of our lives take one line on a tombstone, but the fiction may well fill many volumes. Our choice, in so far as we have one, is not between fiction and fact, but between good and bad fiction. Watergate is bad fiction. Misleading facts and bad

1

fiction govern our lives. If it's a matter of words, if it's a function of language, if it's concerned with what it's like or not like to be human, it will prove to be some sort of fiction.

> We make to ourselves pictures of facts. The picture is a model of reality.

These are words of a philosopher, Ludwig Wittgenstein, but the fiction writer could not have put it better. Writers are picture makers of facts. Their pictures are models of reality.

In the light of this fiction, most of our distinctions are largely a matter of convenience.

What would librarians do without a clear distinction between fiction and nonfiction? What they do is resort to numbers. In this way a distinction that is arbitrary is made to appear perfectly natural. Fiction is over there on the wall to the left, nonfiction to the right.

Those who appreciate facts assume that nonfiction is real in a way that fiction is not. They buy with confidence books of nonfiction: fiction they buy for children and convalescents. Who can say what novels are really about? Nonfiction is plainly about history, about war and peace, house repairs, vitamins, and how to make love. Nonfiction is by nature about something that might prove to be useful. Fiction, if it is good, will often prove to be useless. "What good is reading *that* going to do?" is invariably an unanswerable question. The powers of fiction, as distinct from its uses, are believed to align themselves with the occult, and should be labeled: "Let the Reader Enter at His Own Risk." It has to do with spells, and we are inexperienced with spells for the good.

History, for example, is a good solid subject, but we can print most of the facts on one flap of the jacket. *What* happened and *where* is history—how and why it happened is fiction. If it is good fiction we accept it as history. To have been the general, the soldier, the statesman, the spy in from the cold or one of his victims, is merely to establish the point of view from which fiction can be written. We sense, as we read, that the facts elude us: to have merely been there only adds to our confusion. The small amount of truth we might glean from the report will come about through the shaping of the imagination. The vast fiction of Gibbon persuaded our forefathers that they grasped the decline and fall of Rome. Gibbon read up on Rome, he lived and breathed ruins, he imagined himself and others as Romans, and he wrote the first massive historical novel.

So what about biography? The real life and times of the great and the lowly? In biography the fiction is compounded, since the author presumes to know the unknown, the un-knowable: what the subject felt, what he *actually* thought, what he *really* said. If all this impresses the reader as true, he is reading the work of a good writer of fiction. Anything might be his subject. His problem is to give it the semblance of life.

That still leaves us with autobiography, the honest-to-goodness confessions of the man himself. Cellini and Rousseau, along with numberless others, assure the reader they are sticking to the *facts*. Thoreau tells us:

> I should not talk so much about myself if there were anybody else whom I knew as well.

How sensible that sounds! Each of us a fount of knowledge about ourselves. Montaigne, also, is at pains to assure his readers

> that no man ever treated of a subject that he knew and understood better than I do this that I have taken up: and that in this I am the most learned man alive.

Brave words those! Curious how insistent these fellows are that in speaking of themselves they speak only the facts. It testifies to a deep concern on this subject. Today we know the concern is justified. The man who strains to tell us all, whether Rousseau or Hitler, tells us less what he knows than what his talent makes possible. To confess up a life requires the same imagination it takes to create one. It does if what we confess is a matter of *words*. Where the talent is great, *any* confession is of interest; where it is small or nonexistent, a report from heaven or hell itself will soon have the reader yawning. One reporter on his own life understood that. Goethe described his research into himself as *Truth and Poetry*. It is either truth and poetry or it will prove to be very little.

But there must be *some* facts—what about those documents that record forever the crucial events in human history? Here is one on which the ink is still drying, signaling the cease-fire agreement in Vietnam.

> Immediately after the cease-fire the two South Vietnamese parties will achieve national concord and reconciliation; end hatred and enmity; prohibit all acts of reprisal and discrimination against individuals or organizations that have collaborated with one side or the other; ensure the democratic liberties of the people—personal freedom, freedom of speech, freedom of the press, freedom of meeting, freedom of organization, freedom of political activities, freedom of belief, freedom of movement, freedom of residence, freedom of work, right to property ownership, and right to free enterprise.

The reader of fiction might well feel that this is black humor, a parody of the very concept of a cease-fire. Where facts, of necessity, should have prevailed, we find that fiction has taken flight. In the guise of a treaty the winner-losers devise a contract that declares them winners—wars in which *all* sides are losers are reassembled in this manner. Only fiction—monstrous fiction—makes it possible for a good and just war to prevail.

The compulsion toward fiction is so great among those who believe they are writing *history* that only the self-aware fiction writer should be trusted with the drafts of these statements. He alone, at such moments, knows what fiction is, and what it is not. Not a little of it, described as black humor, is written out of despair of this world as a joke, and not a little of it, admitting to the joke, is written out of the healing need for laughter. The joke is one of the facts writers of nonfiction overlook.

To stick to the facts is a respectable goal, but no writer of interest has long achieved it. Vital statistics are notoriously brief. It is a fact that we are born and die, but in between it is all a tangle of fiction, rounded with a sleep. It is a fact that the President of the United States each year gives a report on the state of the Union. The President, the report, and the Union are facts, but the speech will invariably prove to be fiction, most of it bad. We are long accustomed, having no choice, to this commingling of data and experience, pictures of facts that provide us with false models of reality.

What Good Is It?

Fiction is not the bread of life, nor the wine of life, nor for long the satisfactory *thou* of life, but its hunger mingles with these hungers and is still there when the others are sated. Man dreams before he eats, after he thirsts, and in order to sleep.

Fiction has deep roots, and will not disappear with a change of tools, fashions, or even planets. It provides that link in the chain of awareness that relates man to the ur-mensch of his subconscious. Fiction was there in the dark of the cave, at the beginning, and it will be there in the ruins at the end, oral, chiseled, or computed. It will, because we can't help it. We make fiction like the worm makes silk, but not often so well.

Of this vast production and consumption my concern is

solely with what is written, with deliberation, and marketed as short stories, tall tales, and novels. All of it crafted to please the writer in such a manner that it holds the reader, frequently against his will. This artfully crafted illusion provides literate men with a measure of the shrinkage and expansion of human consciousness, and such a commentary as we have and value on the disordered state of the human soul. It also entertains, distracts, diverts, deludes, corrupts, and cheats.

The sentiment still persists in certain quarters that fiction is also useful, and mightier than the sword. This is an "article of faith" forged in a time of enthusiasm, and not an historical observation. It belongs among the slogans and recommendations for perfume in the arts of love. It has no useful place in the world of facts, but it is secure in the world of fancy. Many book lovers buy it: it is part of their investment in literature.

In point of fact fiction, even at its best, is remarkably useless in the world of events. The man who has read everything is less subject to action than the man who has read nothing. It would be fine to say that fiction maketh a man good, but the evidence is scanty. The inspired fiction of the Bible required Holy sanction to give it authority. That it was "no more" than truth and poetry marked the point of decline in the Book's influence. It is the fear of God, not the love of Truth, that charges the air in the Bible belt. It is the dread of boredom, not the love of life, that stokes the fires of novel consumers. The man with Dante on his tongue, Tolstoi on his mind, goes about his slothful, greedy, covetous, murderous business. The world of Guermantes Way did not lack for fiction, and the butchers of Buchenwald knew their Rilke and Goethe, hummed the arias of Mozart. The men who tinker with rubber, metal, neutrons, and drugs—not those who tinker with fiction—hold the key to events. However, there is always the chance the bad fiction will succeed where the good fails, as in *Mein Kampf*. The limited uses of fiction are perhaps its major asset, linking it with those forces that defy definition, gains that are immaterial, losses beyond accounting, all delights and torments of a private nature, brief candles that flicker in the mind's darkest corners, thereby invaluable. Fiction does play a role in what we call education and weights the arms of girls at the turn of stairways, where young men whose interests are more than literary come to their aid.

Isn't there an oversupply of it already? Why do writers continue to write it?

This is a good question: it should be asked oftener on panel discussions.

Some writers reply that they simply can't help it, like an

itch they must scratch. Others describe it as an addiction acquired in such a manner they can't shake it. Others hardly know why they do it, but appreciate that they are paid for it. It beats working, they say. Still others, well known for their boldness and blunt ways of speaking out on issues, say they write to be famous, or make money, as many do when they sell a movie. This answer has the great virtue of satisfying the people who ask the question. They thought so. Now they are reassured in their thoughts. Among the writers seldom asked, or if asked reluctant to answer, will be found some who write out of talent, and the pleasure talent brings to the writing of fiction. To have a *talent* for fiction is to risk a priesthood where many are called but few are chosen. War and the arts never lack for converts. Talent is also an ear for a distant drummer. It has its romantic side.

> Welcome, O life! I go to encounter for the millionth time the reality of experience and to forge in the smithy of my soul the uncreated conscience of my race.

In the opinion of James Joyce, that is what he was doing. The fiction writer is subject to a sense of mission, and he speaks of conscience rather than truth. A very different writer than Joyce sounds a similar note:

> Man struggles with unborn needs and fulfillment. New unfoldings struggle up in torment in him, as buds struggle

forth from the midst of a plant. Any man of real individuality tries to know and to understand what is happening, even in himself, as he goes along. This struggle for verbal consciousness should not be left out in art. It is a very great part of life. . . . It is the passionate struggle into conscious being.

D. H. Lawrence, too, wanted to be more fully conscious. The word *struggle* dominates his effort toward fulfillment, as it dominates the characters in his novels. What a torment life is! To read Lawrence is to share his struggle for verbal consciousness. Joyce and Lawrence testify to writing as a calling, and the glories and torments of such high endeavor. The slopes of Parnassus are strewn with writers who would have better fulfilled themselves as readers. The contemporary writer, fortunately, is less subject to this romantic agony, and follows Lawrence into life rather than Joyce into exile. He is no longer subject to the superstition that to write well he must give up living, although he will intuit, or soon enough learn, that his muse is not a coy mistress. He has his problems. He will seldom lack something to write about.

In the writer at work the instinct and the ego share a precarious peace. He is at war in his fiction, where a lasting peace is actually possible. Each time the writer creates and solves the problems of fiction, he makes it possible for men and women to live in this world. The manner in which this fiction affirms the world is a measure of its quality: the manner in which it rejects the world is a measure of its fantasy.

Because of the scarcity of novels in the past, the earlier writers of fiction read from the book of life. The modern writer first reads about life in books, and it is fiction that makes him a writer. If he chooses to read all the books that he should, he may well be depressed by their achievement, and shaped to ends that exceed his talents: if he fails to read them he does so at the risk of being ignorant of his calling. *The Waste Land* has been written, *Gatsby* has been written, scores of great and minor writers have sounded the note appropriate to their age and their talent, and on the evidence a state of innocence is of limited use to the writer of novels. He needs must know, even if what he knows is more than he can bear.

None of them knew the color of the sky.

In 1897 this was a new way to open a story. From the reader it required concentration. What was actually being said? It seems the writer's intent is to involve the reader not merely in the reading, but in the writing. It anticipates the thought that the best fiction is increasingly read by writers. It is this that defines it as modern, and contributes to the thralldom of the style. The author means to weave a spell: he is among the hosts of the conjurors.

The pace of this line through the word color is like the striding approach to a takeoff—yet the reader is obliged, with the words *of the sky,* to make a full stop. Who is *them?* Why is the color important? It is what we fail to grasp that both delays and provokes us. This somber tone persists through the paragraph that evokes the scene. Men are at sea in an open boat. Their eyes are fastened on the waves. Crane is a writer who instantly separates the readers of fiction from the idlers. His style includes you in, or blocks you out: turns you on or turns you off. The writing says to the reader, "Look, this is for you," or says it is not. Flaubert made similar demands of the readers who were curious to share Madame Bovary's scandal, but Crane is the first to challenge the reader as a reader.

> None of them knew the color of the sky. Their eyes glanced level, and were fastened upon the waves that swept toward them. These waves were of the hue of slate, save for the tops, which were of foaming white, and all of the men knew the colors of the sea.

Reading these few lines still makes some readers writers, and makes of some writers, for the moment, good readers. Through his *style* the writer achieves maximum self-expression, with a minimum of self-intrusion. To this extent, the style is the man.

Another American shaped the new language to an even more original music. Three years older than Crane, Gertrude Stein is the first of the exiles to see the new world clearer from Paris.

> Romance is the ideal in one's life and it is very lonely living with it lost.

Is this fiction or incantation? The vernacular poetry of Huck Finn is used to sound the natures of three women. *Three Lives* is a book of revelations so artless early readers thought it naïve, although *Melanctha* achieved, without the air of contrivance, the stream-of-consciousness effects we associate with later writers. Great innovators, in the matter of style, influence the writers who, in turn, will charm the public.

> You do not know how long you are in a river when the current moves swiftly. It seems a long time and it may be very short.

This disarming vernacular comes out of *Huck Finn*, but it was Gertrude Stein who revealed to Hemingway the wider range of its possibilities. Through Hemingway, the virus of the vernacular spread world-wide.

Busy at his task of creating the Irish conscience, Joyce listened to a more complex chamber music.

The unwholesome sandflats wanted to suck his treading soles, breathing upward sewage breath.

The concentration of this line, involving all the senses, was written for the hosts of Ireland but largely read by writers. Joyce's example established the emerging practice. The writer learns to write, the reader learns to read. This mystique is the high point in the rise and sanctification of the modern novel as a work of art, a position of such eminence and authority its decline was predictable.

So What's It All About
—This Fiction?

All novels are burdened with the need to make life more interesting than we find it. The means the novelist has to do this are limited, but the reader's appetite is insatiable. He wants something of interest. He seeks something of value. The writer can only confront him with words. Words and more words. The language of fiction can be as plain as a primer:

> It was a quiet night. The swamp was perfectly quiet. Nick stretched under the blanket comfortably. A mosquito hummed close to his ear. Nick sat up and lit a match. The mosquito was on the canvas over his head. Nick moved the match quickly up to it. The mosquito made a satisfactory hiss in the flame.*

* Hemingway

16

Or as artfully elaborate as embroidery:

> The apparition had reached the landing halfway up in our common intensity.*

Or as loose and porous as leafy shade, through which the reader, daydreaming, sees the sky, moving clouds, and is encouraged to write his own fiction.

> The next afternoon Lucy was walking slowly over toward Michigan Avenue. She had never loved the city so much; the city which gave one the freedom to spend one's youth as one pleased, to have one's secret, to choose one's master and serve him in one's own way.†

Such writing distracts the mind from idleness, but does not encourage it to further development.

Good stories are also told, and good fiction is sometimes written, without the deliberate intent of the author. In *Two Years Before the Mast,* Richard Henry Dana chronicled his experience as a common seaman aboard the brig *Pilgrim,* on a voyage around the Cape of Good Hope to California. In his diary we find this comment:

> *Monday, November 10th.* During part of this day we were hove to, but the rest of the time were driving on, under close-reefed sails, with a heavy sea, a strong gale, and frequent squalls of hail and snow.

* Henry James
† Willa Cather

Tuesday, November 11th. The same.
Wednesday. The same.
Thursday. The same.

The repetition of *The same* conveys not only information but experience. This is the way the man at sea apprehends time. Dana reports a death at sea in this manner:

> Death is at all times solemn, but never so much as at sea. A man dies on shore; his body remains with his friends, and the "mourners go about the streets"; but when a man falls overboard at sea and is lost, there is a suddenness in the event, and a difficulty in realizing it, which give to it an air of awful mystery.

This passage has some of the power, as well as the manner, of Donne's *Devotions.* If it is more than a date on a tombstone, death is an experience that defies recording. It is either a bare statement of fact—"Mother died today"—or an experience that must be recreated. These are the powers of the fiction writer, and Dana had them but did not know it. He was trained to be a lawyer. He wrote *Two Years Before the Mast* as a protest against the hard life of the common seaman. Thanks to his talent as a writer, the hard life of common seamen is one of our classics, and we have long lost interest in the protest.

> . . . but one of the finest sights that I have ever seen was an albatross asleep upon the water, during a calm, off Cape

Horn, when a heavy sea was running. There being no breeze, the surface of the water was unbroken, but a long, heavy swell was rolling, and we saw the fellow, all white, directly ahead of us, asleep upon the waves, with his head under his wing; now rising on the top of one of the big billows, and then falling slowly until he was lost in the hollow between.

This reminds us of Melville, and the role Dana played in shaping the imagination Melville took to sea. There are facts in Dana's report, as there are in Melville's, but both survive because they are writers who can shape words to the nature of experience.

The great writers of fiction are those who know what it is, and consider their faculty for it a calling. Life is an excuse for the production of literature. Sixty years after Melville went to sea on the *Acushnet,* Stephen Crane was shipwrecked on his way to Cuba to report on a war. Crane was one of the survivors who ended up in a lifeboat, and shipwreck was the sort of challenge he appreciated. The result was his story "The Open Boat," with the opening lines already quoted. Like Hemingway, he was a good reporter, but only the fully conscious fiction writer achieves the mastery of "The Open Boat." He was not satisfied with *The Red Badge of Courage* because it had not been based on actual experience. His obsession in this matter, like Hemingway's, kept him on the run to wars and places of danger. Only

when he had experienced such facts did he trust his faculty
of shaping them to fiction. This very American confidence in
the facts, rather than the fiction, has persuaded many American writers to feel that if one *gets* the facts why tamper with
them? Crane's "Open Boat" is the answer. Stick to the facts
if you have little talent. If you do have a talent, the facts
plead to be released of their burden of concealed meaning.
And that is the challenge of fiction. A portrait of the artist
as seen in his picture of the facts.

To distinguish good fiction from bad we have nothing but
taste. It registers as a shock of recognition among those for
whom such things really matter.

> I think that I shall never see
> A poem lovely as a tree

impresses many readers as very poetic indeed. It touches on
what they feel about poems and trees. It cannot be satis-
factorily explained why it is sentimental verse, not good
poetry. The same problem exists in prose, where the levels
of taste are equally elusive.

> In there. The words hit me hard. In there was my best
> friend lying on the floor dead. The body. Now I could call
> it that. Yesterday it was Jack Williams, the guy that shared
> the same mud bed with me through two years of warfare in
> the stinking slime of the jungle.

This is fiction by Mickey Spillane, read and appreciated by millions. It has what the reader knows to be "style," in the clipped sentences, the matter-of-fact tone. It is true-to-life for Mike Hammer, and all the Mike Hammer readers. "In there. The words hit me hard." The difference between this writing and the writing it echoes is evident only to the reader who knows the source.

> In the morning it was all over. The fiesta was finished. I woke up about nine o'clock, had a bath, dressed, and went downstairs.

These are lines from *The Sun Also Rises*. His taste shaped by countless Hemingway imitations, the modern reader will find it hard to grasp the initial appeal of the Hemingway style. It seems strained and affected: on occasion simple-minded. This appears to be the fate of a style that seeks an ultimate simplification. If successful, it is soon imitated. Mickey Spillane fans *prefer* Spillane to Hemingway. In this way a great writer, seeking to picture the *facts,* fathers a breed who are content with fantasy projections, using the formula mechanics of the style to display sex, violence, and sadism. All that is required is that sex and violence are known to be *facts.*

Up the ladder a rung we have James Bond. Bond is more "sophisticated" than Hammer, and to this extent his style varies. The creator of Bond, Ian Fleming, faced a problem that was subtle: he wanted to neither insult the intelligence of the reader nor, more important, stimulate it.

> The warehouse was about fifty feet long. Bond slowed and walked softly to the far corner. He flattened himself against the corrugated wall and took a swift look around. . . . A car, a black Lancia Gran Turismo convertible with the hood down, stood beside him, its engine ticking softly. It pointed inland along a deeply tracked dust road.

The introduction of the Gran Turismo is as obtrusive and mechanical as Spillane's devices but Fleming hopes that the high style of the car will conceal the low caliber of the writing. The key to Bond is *softly*. The characters are still good guys and bad guys, but they are smart enough to affect sophisticated tastes in women and art.

The crucial step upward for such fiction concerns the reader's intelligence. Bond appeals to it, but does not involve it, a flawless resolution. He can be and is read between the hamburger and the cup of coffee. Time passes smoothly that good fiction is intended to stop.

In this way we proceed by degrees of craft sophistication toward an optimum level of fictive reality. The reader may have observed these steps in himself, and think back with amusement on the books he read that he thought "true-to-life." Even Hemingway seems mannered and artificial to those who have toughened their gums on Tolkien and science fiction. Kahlil Gibran is now back in vogue as a guru. This is all part of a new "picture of the facts" seen by those who have turned their backs on the old.

> But suppose one dislikes all this theatre of the soul? I too find it tiresome to have to meet it so often and in such familiar forms. . . . The Self may think it wears a gay new ornament, delightfully painted, but from outside we see that it is a millstone. Or again, this personality of which the owner is so proud is from the Woolworth store, cheap tin or plastic from the five-and-dime of souls. Seeing it in this way, a man may feel that being human is hardly worth the trouble.

This cry from Bellow's Sammler comprehends a reality that is not so easily captured by crafty verbal refinements on the familiar, outdated models. Hemingway externalized in order to simplify, to impose a moment of order on disordered movements: Bellow internalizes to achieve a maximum complexity of impressions that are real-seeming to Sammler. It is a strain on Sammler, as it is to the reader, to admit to the variety and chaos of this theatre of the soul. Most people are prepared to ask questions, and make many demands, but not to inquire why they should be human. This is an aspect of the new true-to-life of which the old had little suspicion. Aren't there enough problems? Did this Sammler have to come up with *that*? It is of interest that Sammler, a mensch of the old world, is the instrument Bellow chose to sound the range of the new world, where skepticism concerning the man who *thinks* is considered sound novelistic practice. Sammler's problem is to make *room* for the facts—one that requires great imagination—rather than contrive a style that will make the old facts seem more convincing. He comprehends a reality in which the partisan enthusiasms of the young and the old are acknowledged to be part of the true-to-life torment, a model of reality with which they both must come to terms. This larger-than-life illusion is available only in good fiction, and makes possible to those who seek, and can bear it, a suitable model of how things really are.

Touching on a Few of the Fine Points

If it's a matter of taste, can good fiction be explained, or merely recognized?

> Mother died today. Or, maybe, yesterday; I can't be sure.

The signature of the writer, like spoor traces, can be detected in a phrase, or the tracks of a sentence. A writer who reads this line may want to pause there, rather than lose it. The character of Meursault is summed up in it. Much that follows is by way of elaboration. This is the kernel. The writer may settle for the virus of the suggestion.

Written in French, then translated into English, Samuel Beckett speaks in this manner through *Molloy*:

> Let me try and explain. From things about to disappear I turn away in time. To watch them out of sight, no, I can't do it.

To analyze this "style" does not explain it. It has the unmistakable stamp of the author, and casts his spell. We might also observe that it is better in small doses than large ones.

A single line, like a phrase in music, may indicate a writer's key, his pervading tone, which the trained ear can detect throughout the writer's fiction—but to appreciate the nature of his music we need a little more.

> Generous tears filled Gabriel's eyes. He had never felt like that himself towards any woman, but he knew that such a feeling must be love. The tears gathered more thickly in his eyes and in the partial darkness he imagined he saw the form of a young man standing under a dripping tree. Other forms were near. His soul had approached that region where dwell the vast hosts of the dead. He was conscious of, but could not apprehend, their wayward and flickering existence. His own identity was fading out into a grey impalpable world: the solid world itself, which these dead had one time reared and lived in, was dissolving and dwindling.

This is Joycean chamber music from his story "The Dead," more tender and melodic than was customary, but characteristic of his best effects, his "epiphanies." In this passage, written in Trieste, he looked back with affection on his past in Dublin, and found it tolerable. Joyce doesn't hesitate to play on the reader's emotions—the key emotion-packed words thicken the passage like raisins: *love, soul, hosts of the dead*—and the invocation is free of his customary mockery. He shares Gabriel's sentiments, and openly offers them to the reader. The romantic side of Joyce, his taste for Pater's verbal music, the appeal of a scene that verges on the tearful, are given full sway in a manner that Joyce would not return to. Nowhere else is he so openly vulnerable.

> There was grace and mystery in her attitude as if she were a symbol of something. He asked himself what is a woman standing on the stairs in the shadow, listening to distant music, a symbol of. If he were a painter, he would paint her in that attitude. Her blue felt hat would show off the bronze of her hair against the darkness and the dark panels of her skirt would show off the light ones. *Distant Music* he would call the picture if he were a painter.

In D. H. Lawrence, the possibilities afforded by altering the syntax are of little interest. We sense the author's presence in the scene's immediacy and his word choice. It is always the extremes of emotion that Lawrence's characters experience, sometimes within the same sentence.

> One morning the sisters were sketching by the side of Willey Water, at the remote end of the lake. Gudrun had waded out to a gravelly shoal, and was seated like a Buddhist, staring fixedly at the water plants that rose succulent from the mud of the low shores. What she could see was mud,

soft, oozy, watery mud, and from its festering chill, water-plants rose up, thick and cool and fleshy, very straight and turgid, thrusting out their leaves at right angles, and having dark lurid colours, dark green and blotches of black-purple and bronze. But she could feel their turgid fleshy structure as in a sensuous vision, she *knew* how they rose out of the mud, she *knew* how they thrust out from themselves, how they stood stiff and succulent against the air.

There is no one comparable to Lawrence, so he takes some getting used to. If the reader reads well, he is soon exhausted. In Lawrence the characters lead lives as intense as the gods'. No writing is so simultaneously charged with the appearance of life and its transformation, the mind of Lawrence at the same moment involved with observation and creation. Where other writers observe nature, the juices of nature are within Lawrence, as the swooping hawk is within Tolstoi. He is not for everyone. But everyone should make that choice for himself.

The man who feels and thinks as intensely as Lawrence can be tiresome to normal mortals as a daily companion, but he provides the expanding experience that makes intense living possible. Both Joyce and Lawrence insisted on being "true-to-life." Each put real people into their fiction, and were scrupulously honest about details—"the ineluctable modality of the visible."* Neither, however, ever imagined

* James Joyce

that the true life could be captured without "talent," a faculty deriving from the imagination. Hemingway's impression of a bullfight is accurate in a way that Lawrence is not accurate, but Lawrence's impressions of the faces of love are accurate in a way that is unknown to Hemingway. Their individual gifts and faculties have their special virtues and limitations. Each can only give us one model of reality.

Thomas Mann's special gift is that of a double vision, the way the particular evokes and represents the universal, the mythic.

> Once the lad [Tadziu] was summoned to speak to a guest who was waiting for his mother at their cabin. He ran up, ran dripping wet out of the sea, tossing his curls, and put out his hand, standing with his weight on one leg, resting the other foot on the toes; as he stood there in a posture of suspense the turn of his body was enchanting, while his features wore a look half shamefaced, half conscious of the duty breeding laid upon him to please.

To these representations of reality Hemingway contributed the American picture.

> They hanged Sam Cardinella at six o'clock in the morning in the corridor of the county jail. The corridor was high and narrow with tiers of cells on either side. All the cells were occupied. The prisoners had been brought in for the hanging. Five men sentenced to be hanged were in the five top cells. Three of the men to be hanged were negroes. They

were very frightened. One of the white men sat on his cot with his head in his hands. The other lay flat on his cot with a blanket wrapped around his head.

The artifice of this passage may seem obvious to a new generation of readers, but to those who were the first to read it it seemed to capture life itself. The true-to-fiction had suddenly become the true-to-life.

The examples I have quoted show the wide variety of each writer's model of reality, but they all have in common respect for the true-to-life. Each in his fashion seeks to convince the reader that he describes things as he sees them. Of the four, Hemingway is the most successful in implying that he describes things as they are. This was the explicit purpose of his style, and many writers and readers alike felt that the "gap" between literature and life had narrowed. Perhaps the very fact that it *appeared* to have narrowed persuaded writers to feel that it no longer existed. If they lived a little harder, observed a little closer, talked a little plainer, they might lay their hands on experience itself, and put to rest their long, gnawing obsession to possess life.

In point of fact, the true-to-life can only be true to the prevailing reality concept. No ultimate reality will be evoked by cracking barriers or talking plainer. These are but props of the familiar scene, shifted around somewhat to create a new effect. The Zen master is closer to what remains elusive than is the novelist who pants after the ultimate.

All our finalizations—*once and for all time,* etc.—prove to be temporary at the moment they are made, although their effect at the time can be bracing. It is a wondrous fact that the art of painting, stimulated but not coerced by the photographic image, abandoned the true-to-life esthetic at the moment the novelist accepted it as a goal. Strange paradox that the craft of artful lying should aspire to a photographic likeness! Or is it all of one piece, once we determine to counterfeit life with words? Joyce's Gabriel, Lawrence's Gudrun, Mann's Tadziu, and Hemingway's camera eye provide pictures of reality according to the writer's needs and gifts.

Fiction As Truth Maker
and Life Enhancer

The first fiction of our lives is that of dreaming: in our dreams we are creators and consumers of fiction. To sleep well we must dream. Dreaming is part of the chemistry of life. The savage dances a wakeful dream, and dreams keep us in touch with a distant drummer. Wakeful dreaming is a truth-making process that structures the airy mansions of the soul. Poets strike this chord so often we have come to ignore what is being said. In dreams begin responsibilities: in fiction we find their implications and resolutions.

The fiction writer cannot, at one and the same time, be equally true to life and to his emerging fiction. Character and scene elicit from the writer more than he wills, and more than he knows. The measure of this "more" is his creative contribution. He writes to discover what he is thinking, not to tell us how little or how much he knows.

When we are asked—or when we ask ourselves—to "face the facts," we are usually at a loss to determine what they are. D. H. Lawrence had a consuming passion for the facts of life. The torment and fever of much of his writing is his effort to get at them. To write a good poem, to read a good novel, to be moved by music, to be warmed by affection, are ultimate goods that are good in themselves. They seek to gratify what is otherwise immeasurable.

The long, demon-like beast lashed out again, spread on the air as if it were flying, looking something like a dragon, then closing up again, inconceivably powerful and explosive. The man's body, strung to its efforts, vibrated strongly. Then a sudden sharp, white-edged wrath came up in him. Swift as lightning he drew back and brought his free hand down like a hawk on the neck of the rabbit. Simultaneously, there came the unearthly abhorrent scream of a rabbit in the fear of death. It made one immense writhe, tore his wrists and his sleeves in a final convulsion, all its belly flashed white in a whirlwind of paws, and then he had slung it round and had it under his arm, fast. It cowered and skulked. His face was gleaming with a smile.

"You wouldn't think there was all that force in a rabbit," he said, looking at Gudrun. And he saw her eyes black as night in her pallid face, she looked almost unearthly. The scream of the rabbit, after the violent tussle, seemed to have torn the veil of her consciousness.

33

This passage from *Women in Love* does just that—it tears the veil of conventional consciousness and leaves the living flesh and nerves exposed. The scene is calculated to reveal the concealed streak of cruelty in Gudrun, as well as in the author and the reader. It is all a matter of revelation, and not many early readers found it life-enhancing. The enhancement is the mind's gratification of a truth revealed that is usually concealed, not to be confused with the feeling of uplift provided by good works. The distinction cannot be formulated, and forever distinguishes between types of readers. One is pleased and enhanced, one is disturbed and depressed, by what is revealed. It is Lawrence's gift to provide his readers with pleasure and torment in intense proportions. The life enhancement he provides is unique, as is also his life criticism. No one excelled his intuition in matters of the life in life, and what is dead in life. He could be cruel, thrashing out like the rabbit to tear the veils of unawareness. His example provides us with clear distinctions in the fuzzy areas of life and art, life and literature.

All of Tolstoi's moral tales are less life-enhancing than this moment of truth in "The Death of Ivan Ilych":

Ivan Ilych looks at her [his wife], scans her all over, sets against her the whiteness and plumpness and cleanness of her hands and neck, the gloss of her hair, and the sparkle of her vivacious eyes. He hates her with all his soul. And

34

the thrill of hatred he feels for her makes him suffer from her touch.

No reassuring moral insight here, merely the head-clearing carbolic whiff of truth. An insight, a revelation in Tolstoi's mind at the moment of writing this scene, not to be confused with a shrewd observation. It was surely repugnant to Tolstoi's morals, but the truth of it thrilled the artist in him, and both disturbs and gratifies the reader.

"Ivan Ilych" is the story of a man dying, a man in continual despair, and that is hard to make life-enhancing. That it is at all possible lies in the fact that man can still choose between truth and falsehood, and this freedom of choice *is* life-enhancing. In facing the fact of his own mortality, Tolstoi faces a truth that is dreaded by all men. Ivan Ilych recalls the syllogism he learned as a boy: "Caius is a man, men are mortal, therefore Caius is mortal," and how this had always impressed him as a truth about Caius, but certainly not about himself.

That Caius—man in the abstract—was mortal was perfectly correct, but he [Ivan] was not Caius, not an abstract man, but a creature quite, quite separate from all the others. He had been little Vanya, with a mamma and a papa, with Mitya and Volodya, with the toys, a coachman and a nurse, afterwards with Katenka and with all the joys, griefs, and delights of childhood, boyhood, and youth. . . .

Ivan's appetite for life has always exceeded his relatively modest interest in truth, but confronted with death there is something in his soul that will no longer tolerate deception. This love of truth we acknowledge to be life-enhancing, although the truth it admits to is death. Nothing so cleaved the soul of Tolstoi as this intolerable fact, his appetite for life equal to, and often exceeding, his passion for truth. "Ivan Ilych" is the scene for this fatal confrontation, and draws from Tolstoi this tormented compromise:

> "It is finished!" someone said near him.
> He heard these words and repeated them in his soul.
> "Death is finished," he said to himself. "It is no more!"
> He drew in a breath, stopped in the midst of a sigh, stretched out, and died.

We are not as moved by this revelation as we were by the Caius incident. Is it that we sense the soul of Tolstoi hedging, in this ultimate confrontation, as he did not hedge when Ivan observed his wife? Ivan Ilych, in any case, leaves to the reader Tolstoi's unresolved enigma—whether the passion for truth is or is not to triumph over his desire for eternal life.

Paradoxically, a sense of life enhancement based on *hope* is more difficult to achieve than one based on doubt. We are secretly prepared to believe the worst, and hearing it, we are relieved to admit it. Of the hopeful we are privately, in our heart of hearts, skeptical. The seamy side of life is so well documented we need look nowhere else but to the novel for it, and where life departs from such convincing fiction it seems unreal. Writers who are by nature optimistic and sanguine often have a hard time convincing skeptical readers that the top side of life is as real as the bottom. We *want* to believe it, and wanting to believe is the source of our doubt.

In Camus's *Notebooks* we find this notation:

Characters.
The old man and his dog. Eight years of hatred.

From this seed we have the scene of Salamano and his dog in *The Stranger*.

One of his mates on the railway whose bitch had just had pups had offered him one, and he had taken it, as a companion. He'd had to feed it from the bottle at first. But, as a dog's life is shorter than a man's, they'd grown old together, so to speak.

"He was a cantankerous brute," Salamano said. "Now and then we had some proper set-tos, he and I. But he was a good mutt all the same."

I said he looked well bred, and that evidently pleased the old man.

"Ah, but you should have seen him before his illness!" he said. "He had a wonderful coat; in fact, that was his best point, really. I tried hard to cure him; every mortal night after he got that skin disease I rubbed an ointment in. But the real trouble was old age, and there's no curing that."

Camus is not a poet of hatred. In his hands, we have a relationship that mingles the poignant and the pathetic, and is at once an affliction and life-enhancing. The existential truths of Sartre's *Nausea*, Beckett's *Godot*, and Camus's *Myth of Sisyphus* are now the accepted "truths" of the college graduate student.

The Problem

Literature and Life was the title of a heavy volume I once carried on my daily commute to high school in Chicago. It began with *Beowulf* and advanced to Walter Pater. It had the wisdom to stop on the fringe of the present and avoid dilemmas that have no resolution. The past existed. I saw its bearded giants in niches on the stairs, or installed in the arch of the auditorium. The present was the little I observed around me, most of it remarkably lifelike. I lived in the slums on the near North Side, but I commuted to a high school several miles north. That was the future: like Gatsby, I hankered for a better life. On my commute I read from *Literature and Life,* which sometimes shortened the trip, sometimes stretched it out. The literature of the book spanned a thousand years: the life was my own. This was not a clear distinction I made at the time, but one that came to me many years later. In my boyhood I had been Tom Sawyer. In Chicago I hoped to be Stover at Yale. Sometimes I grasped such distinctions quite clearly, and knew that Douglas Fairbanks was *not* the Black Pirate, and that I was not, in spite of all we had in common, either Robin Hood or Sir Gawain. I was great for Sir Gawain. What he defined for me were possibilities.

Sir Gawain and the Green Knight shared my mind on equal footing with Al Capone, a villain whose influence dominated the south pole of my commute. Larrabee and Blackhawk, then known as Death's Corner, was twenty yards to the south of the Larrabee YMCA, where the rattle of gunfire sometimes competed with the bounce and roll of billiard balls. I was employed by the "Y" to help soothe the young and savage breast. To my assembled young hoodlums, fresh from a slot-machine raid, or to a bivouac of blanket-draped small fry locally identified as Friendly Indians, I would recite Sir Gawain's speech to his tempter, or the more gripping scene where the giant Green Knight, beheaded by Sir Gawain, rides off with his own head into the forest, passages that I freshly memorized on my daily commute. The green mind has the power, greater than the mature one, to live in these opposing worlds and still function. With the aggressive *thereness* of our environment, packaged into parcels of specialization (the urban, the rural, the depressed, etc.), the presentiment grows that facts will be found wherever we peel away the encrustations of fiction. If we probe, or scrape, or dig deep enough (we believe), we will come to facts.

The relationship of literature to life is that of education to adult experience—the palmy days of one's youth are over, and one begins the serious business of living. To the business of living, fiction exists as an escape. To close the gap between literature and life the writer schooled himself in the observable facts, the facts proving to be of more interest than the fiction. As the writer grew bolder, and the life tougher, literature receded as life approached. Understandably, the writer came to feel that with a little more effort life could be grasped without the intervention of fiction. This is an old obsession, not a new one, and has the endorsement of many great talents. Thoreau believed it, Whitman believed it, and numberless writers have put the belief into practice. To dispense with the artifices of the novel, to describe no more nor less than what one sees, what one knows, is the predictable climax of the realistic tradition. Such a writer must believe that what he *sees,* and what he *knows,* are easily rendered into language. He must be free of the doubt that this *rendering* is inescapably a process of fiction, and that his solid-seeming words are merely pictures of the facts.

The writer's passion for "the facts," free of all fictive intervention, is perhaps as old as the craft of fiction, as is his desire for a language free of inherited affectations. American writers found such a language in the American vernacular. It is hardly strange that after a century of its use we have our own standards of appraising fiction, and just naturally assume that if we are true-to-life we are also true-to-fiction. That fiction must also be true to itself has been lost in this transformation. Didn't it set out to be true-to-life, and isn't that what it is? The history of this doctrine is now so entrenched it constitutes a creed below the level of discussion, but for both the writer and the reader of fiction it is important to grasp how this happened. The *facts,* so called, are in: the imagination is out.

On Being
True-to-Life

From Homer to the present, the need to tell it like it is is a line of descent of both fiction and nonfiction, the skeptics among the listeners being the first to recognize that fiction is a form of artful lying. This reader saw through much that he heard about Odysseus, and he sees through much that he reads about Herzog. A major problem of craft is how "to take such a reader in." How to make fiction, that is, true-to-life.

From the first it was recognized that the *lower* the life, the truer it seemed. Even Dante, out of his mind for Heaven, sensed that Hell was more photogenic, both Hell and Purgatory providing a better mirror for life on earth. Neither is Hell so long absent from common daily experience that the writer should lack a public. The craft of fiction is that branch of the arts where what the author *perceives* is more important than what he observes. This is a nice, but crucial, distinction, like the one that separates the men from the boys.

That April is the cruelest month startled most readers, lying outside the range of their weather observations, but some accept it as true-to-life perception. As simple as it seems, the question still arises: What is true-to-life? *Whose* life, for example?

> Dear Dr. Schoenfeld:
> I am a 13 year old chick, who 4 days ago lost my virginity. The dude I balled and I were very stoned, and I didn't come. Do you think I should get a VD test?

That is an inquiry in the morning paper. We can assume it is true to the person who wrote it: a writer of fiction would quote it verbatim. How improve, he would ask, on life itself? At this point, and on this level, the vernacular seems to achieve the representation of the facts the writer desires.

> Then the 47 year old housewife of a $500 a month San Jose shoe salesman took a deep breath and talked about the checkered past of her "good daughter," who gave birth to an illegitimate son when she was 19, turned topless dancer before she was 20, fell in with motorcycle gang members believed to be associated with the Manson family, and now stands charged with murder. "I can't blame her for what's happened—not really," her mother said.

This too is a report from the newspaper, unsullied by the craft of fiction. Is this an instance of life imitating art? The writer of black humor could contribute little to the portrait. For writing of comparable interest we have to turn to "good" fiction. Here is J. D. Salinger's Holden Caulfield:

> If you really want to hear about it, the first thing you'll probably want to know is where I was born, and what my lousy childhood was like, and how my parents were occupied and all before they had me, and all that David Copperfield kind of crap, but I don't feel like going into it, if you want to know the truth.

Do we want to know the truth? This fictional comment shares with the nonfiction I've quoted the vernacular tone of the *real* experience, of the true-to-life. Why is it that with each passing year the real seems to be nearer the bottom of the barrel? Is it a matter of taste, a matter of talent, or is it chiefly a matter of language that whacking off comes easier to Alex Portnoy than it did to Holden Caulfield? What is it, if not the language, that makes his remarkable complaint so attractive? He really tells us very little, but he tells us all about whacking off. Only the vernacular would prove to be equal to this awesome task. Only the reader of considerable sophistication would know that the candor of Holden Caulfield differs from that of the young lady writing to Dr. Schoenfeld, but it is not a difference that will turn her from life to literature for advice. It is Dr. Schoenfeld's opinion she wants, not that of J. D. Salinger. Since we lack a bona-fide detached reality to which we might turn as a basis of judgment, we are left with a true-to-life established by life, with strong fictive elements, and a true-to-life established by fiction, with strong lifelike elements. Which is the *truer* remains a matter of the reader's taste.

Although bad fiction appears to rule our lives, and proves to be more influential than "good" fiction, the writer and reader of good fiction sustain the illusion that fiction is truer to the life that "matters," the rest of life being real enough but lacking consciousness of what it is, and what it might be. Mike Hammer is real, in his fashion, but only good fiction knows what is real about him, and what is false. The daily use and abuse of the "vernacular tongue," its artful honing by both those who use it and those who write it, has blurred the once clear-cut distinction between life and its mirrored reflection. The world and its image are seen as one. The "style" that gives us this assurance is a craft achievement so invisible it appears to be absent, persuading the reader that life and the lifelike, with a little patience, will appear as one. The look of life, the tone and timbre of life, is increasingly one seamless vernacular fabric, comprehending how we sound: "The dude I balled"; how we think: "If you really want to hear about it"; and how we think we feel: "The great thing is to last and to get your work done and see and hear and learn and understand."* When this tone is persuasive, artfully artless, we are easily convinced that the lifelike is true-to-life.

"The Americans," Whitman prophesied, "are going to be the most fluent and melodious-voiced people in the world— and the most perfect users of words. The new world, the new times, the new vistas need a new tongue . . . what is more, they will have a new tongue—will not be satisfied until it is evolved." This new tongue is approaching its moment of triumph, but it has consequences Whitman did not imagine. We have the new world, the new times, the new vistas, but the grain of the vernacular *naturally* slopes downward. It is the fountainhead of what comes naturally, but it is reluctant to respond to effort. The writer feels that, the reader feels it, and the writer is reluctant to go against it. The language leads, and the writer follows where it leads.

How did this come to pass? Aren't we the dreamers who taught the world to fly?

There is a lag of thirty years between Whitman's exhortation and the voice of Huck Finn.

> Two or three days and nights went by; I reckon I might say they swum by, they slid along so quiet and smooth and lovely. Here is the way we put in the time.

* Hemingway

Here the language leads the writer, and the reader, into territory that is new. The writer himself is uncertain of the terrain, and the spell of enchantment he is under. Is it a real world, really true-to-life, or a fantasy true to Huck Finn only? The point is not resolved, nor does the author comprehend the novelty of the situation. He is a sensible writer of frontier humor, well known for a story about a leaping frog. He is profoundly moved to write about the past, but never long clear *how* to write about it. Over the seven-year period of composition his point of view and "voice" vacillated, appropriate to a person whose voice was about to change. Although the narrative wavers, Huck Finn is the first of the American boys to tell the adults how it really is.

A writer half Twain's age, but more certain of his intent, wrote about a youth's initiation to war.

Once the line encountered the body of a dead soldier. He lay upon his back staring at the sky. He was dressed in an awkward suit of yellowish brown. The youth could see that the soles of his shoes had been worn to the thinness of writing paper, and from a great rent in one the dead foot projected piteously. And it was as if fate had betrayed the soldier. In death it exposed to his enemies that poverty which in life he had perhaps concealed from his friends.

There is nothing here of lyrical charm: the writer's eye is for paradox and details. The young author had never experienced a war, but he thought it an interesting challenge to describe one as if he had. Huck Finn, remembered by a man who was aging, and *The Red Badge of Courage*, conjured up by a youth whose writing preceded his experience, had in common a language appropriate to their separate needs.

Two years after Crane died, in exile in England, Gertrude Stein left Baltimore to settle in Paris. Living in Paris may have helped her to see clearly the life she knew in Baltimore.

> Anna looked very well this day. She was always very careful in her dress and sparing of new clothes. She made herself always fulfill her own ideal of how a girl should look when she took her Sundays out. Anna knew so well the kind of ugliness appropriate to each rank of life.

Would we say that this language leads the writer, or that what is new in the language is being led? We sense, immediately, that it serves a new and inscrutable purpose.

> Sometimes the thought of how all her world was made, filled the complex, desiring Melanctha with despair.

The content of this statement would prove to be inseparable from the manner of speaking. *Feeling* is what matters, and Gertrude Stein's craft is the first to limit itself to that subject. Of all fiction, it is the least concerned with data, major issues, speculation, epic or mythic, or other vast manipulations to make the modern world possible in art, characteristic obsessions of her male contemporaries.

Some of the early readers of Stein's fiction thought the author well intentioned but perhaps simple-minded, not grasping what it is that constitutes literature. Those who grasped what Stein was up to experienced a peculiarly intense captivity. Sherwood Anderson and Hemingway were among the first to spread the virus of her infection. It might not be clearly grasped *what* she was doing, but how she was doing it proved to be contagious. Simple words, the rhythms of common speech deliberately made uncommon, apprehend a way of feeling, a way of seeing, and in the fullness of time a way of being, a life style. Predictably, we can say with hindsight, this all-American celebration was appropriately staged in exile. The triumph of Stein is that of the emerging vernacular. Joyce, Mann, and Proust mark a summing up, *Three Lives* an inexhaustible beginning. In fifty years she is still little read, but she is known around the world through her converts. At long last (it appeared), what had begun with Homer, and persisted through numberless mutations, would quite logically achieve its flowering in the barbaric yawp of the new world, a babble of tongues its writers of talent would make melodious. The ultimate realism, the ultimate true-to-life, and the ultimate public for this production was merely a matter of telling it like it is while writing as you pleased.

A volume by that title, *I Write As I Please,* was actually published in the early thirties, reporting on the author's travels in communist Russia. At the same time, a Frenchman, writing as he pleased, published his travels in *Journey to the End of the Night.* The American sought to describe the facts of life, the Frenchman the other side of life. No parallel journey was taken by an American—with the exception of Agee's *Let Us Now Praise Famous Men*—but the American writer believed life would be different: the Frenchman knew it would not.

The American language was well prepared for Céline, but not the American mind. His surreal blend of fiction, fantasy, and fact, the hallucinated aspect of his daylight vision, were experienced by Americans as shock waves from a remote continental disturbance, not part of the new wave of the future.

In the great hazy desert around a town, where its luxury, ending in rottenness and slime, is proved to be a lie, the town presents its posterior among the dustbins for all who wish to see. There are some factories one avoids walking past: they give out every sort of smell, some of them almost unbelievable, and the surrounding air can stink no more. Close by, a little traveling fair moulders between two tall chimneys of unequal height, its wooden horses too costly for rachitic urchins, picking their noses, who sometimes for weeks on end long to ride them, attracted, repelled and fascinated all at once by their abandoned air, poverty, and the music.

That is a barbaric yawp Whitman did not dream of shouting over the roofs of the world.

We shall never be at peace [Céline said] until everything has been said, once for all time. . . .

Whether true or not, this statement left a memorable impression on many writers, some of them American. In its simplicity it acquired the weight and persuasion of a doctrine. Céline had in mind the human condition, as distinct from the literary situation: what he had to say proved to be too strong for American tastes. It gave little thought to form, and explicitly violated existing notions of style. Céline is not the first writer of genius to abandon literary preconceptions and replace them with his own model of the true-to-life. The writer's passion for life, free of fictive intervention, derives from the example of all writers of fiction who achieve a new picture of the facts. Céline did. Great writers of fiction do: it is a function of their talent. It will not prove to be true that everything has been said, but we shall not be at peace without it. True-to-life becomes fiction where it perceives more than it observes.

A Triumph—and
Its Consequences

The word *vernacular,* in the Latin, means belonging to "home-born slaves." Home-born slaves in the South, home-born ruffians in the slums, home-born and -raised pioneers on the frontier spoke a language that departed in wondrous ways from the "written" language of the popular novel. The "vernacular" was "funny," or savagely grotesque, as in the capers and likker brawls of Mike Fink. Frontier farce may have promoted, more than it relieved, the violence of men who were boys at heart, but the rawness of this yawp delayed its appearance in "literature."

At this time photography provided the writer with the assurance of an objective, irreducible reality he needed merely the talent, and the candor, to describe. To these writers it seemed reasonable to conclude that an accurate rendering of what was "real" fulfilled the possibilities of fiction. Writers of divergent talents and opinions felt the impact of the new doctrine. James Joyce, the great technician of language, assembled models of reality that were at once an inspiration and a frustration. How go beyond him? What did he leave to be done? Not everybody was inhibited by Joyce's example, since the scale of his achievement put him *au-dessus de la mêlée*. American writers were less given to theory and more reliant on talent and intuition. Although amateurs compared to Joyce, they were the first to intuit (through Stein's example) that the catchall web of the vernacular reflected the mind at its conscious level. This new melodious tongue shaped the writer to a greater extent than he shaped the language. To that extent he was more its servant than its master, and more inclined to follow it than to lead it. This confidence in the language had the effect of depressing the imagination. It appeared to be the very nature of the language to provide the writer with what he needed. Every day it was new. Keeping up with the language was keeping abreast of life. The extent to which this was, and is, true nourishes a very lively and infectious fiction. The movies, the TV, pundits, entertainers were of one language and one imagination compact. One or two novels might set the pace, but most of them were following the example. It takes time to write *and* publish a novel— in that passage of time the novel may have become a cliché. The *use* of the cliché is one of the subtler crafts of fiction, but it refers the author back to his imagination, a faculty that is often rusty with disuse. He has learned to do without it. He has come to question the nature of its role in fiction. Wasn't it possible that *fiction* owed its existence to a scarcity of facts?—and when the facts were more than adequate the fiction might be dispensed with? Wasn't this apparent in the blurring distinction between the fiction and the author? Tom Wolfe would prove to be Tom Wolfe. Hemingway, Hemingway. Good writing need not exclude a certain artifice, but the emphasis had shifted to personal history on a factual level. The reliance was on what factually existed, rather than what remained to be imagined. In this new fact-fiction hybrid there would be problems of taste, problems of libel, and in the long run problems of fiction, but were these details important if the writer was coming to terms with "life"? If he had finally brought life, that is, to his own terms?

To some readers it now seems that the mania to "tell all" serves other causes than those of "freedom." The individual human being, as we know him, is an assemblage of millennia-won distinctions that reach their climax in the concept of what is private, and the negation of what is private is the liquidation of the individual. In its natural state, before artful tampering, the vernacular embodies the aggregate consciousness, and one voice will more than suffice to tell it like it is.

The language leads, and we continue to follow where it leads. At its inception, as Whitman predicted, this practice liberated the imagination. The writer felt that he had gained free access to a vast and unexploited continent, comparable to a view of the plains from the eastern bluffs of the Missouri. Everywhere he gazed, including within himself, he confronted unexploited lodes of material. Raw life. Life that awaited the writer's recognition. Not a few of them reeled with intoxication, providing an instructive example for others. It was too big to gulp. Better take a piece of it at a time. A stretch on the river, a settlement on the prairie, sons and daughters of the middle border, pillars of cloud on the receding horizon, and right there in the heart of the family, giants in the earth. Both writers and homesteaders were encouraged to stake out their claims in the manner of the land rush. Western writers, Southern writers, Rocky Mountain and Northwest Territory writers, Dreiser's Chicago, Anderson's Ohio, Lewis's Main Steet, Hemingway's Big Two-Hearted River, Faulkner's Yoknapatawpha County, and Eliot's mythic Waste Land, comprehending the Missouri on the west and the Thames on the east. Writers were easily identified with a region, and the region became a school of writing. The largest of these provinces, and the last to be discovered, was the submerged world of black Americans, custom-designed to be accepted, exploited, and invisible.

The assumption that life is sufficient unto itself, if boldly gazed upon and fearlessly recorded, is an impression that we owe equally to realism in fiction and to what is documentary in movies. In the main, it is a reassuring sensation, and we should be grateful for it. Understandably, the writer schooled in this practice will have little recourse to his imagination— to the faculty, in its infancy, that led him to write. An obsession with craft effects may well blind him to craft limitations. The role of imaginative freedom is sacrificed to explicit verbal freedoms. This will not silence a first-rate creative talent, but it will depress the very faculty that requires the greatest cultivation, and hasten the blight of his premature retirement. Fitzgerald touchingly speaks of his lack of experience when compared with Hemingway, who recouped his used-up resources by turning to wars, bullfights, and safaris. It is amazing that Fitzgerald, one of the most self-aware of his generation of writers, should accept rather than examine this all-American superstition. A reader of Joyce, Mann, and Proust, it did not occur to him to ask how this practice tallied with these writers of genius, none of whom were great athletes, war reporters, or tireless hunters of lions and women. In the American mind, and in the American language, experience and exposure count for more than talent, and are more accessible to the reader.

This commitment to language is not new—every innovator is subject to it—but seldom before have life and language appeared to be one encompassing, seamless fabric; the language the happening in which we all participate. Norman Mailer's large talent uses it as the basis of his confrontations. His dilemma seems to be twofold: to be more than Norman Mailer, and to write more than a novel. His book *The Armies of the Night* is subtitled *History as a Novel* and *The Novel as History*. The "predicament" of the novel is stated, and both the reader and the writer are offered an option. If it's fiction you want, here is some fiction: if it's facts, here are some facts. Mailer's example comprehends the rise and the crisis of the vernacular vision. The vernacular itself constitutes a model of reality. But if the facsimile of life is what we have always wanted, why is it that we still seem to lack it? Or why, having what it is we want, we are still dissatisfied.

The nonfiction of John Hersey, such as *Hiroshima,* provided scrupulous examples of writing *as* history, free of the familiar liberties of fiction. Hersey achieved this true-to-history illusion by remaining all but invisible himself, a conjuring act that is quite beyond the remarkable gifts of Mr. Mailer. Mailer's novel-as-history must make room for

Mailer, since it would not be much without him. The enlargement we sense in the format is due to the presence of the author, and we measure his success by *his* measure. If we examine what is there besides Mailer, we see that the method is not so new—what we have is the format of a large and original talent. Writers not so generously endowed, however, should not be encouraged to believe that in *not* writing a novel they are writing something larger. In being false to fiction, are we, ipso facto, true-to-life? In being true-to-life what are we true to? It is seldom if ever the heart's affections, and even less the truths of the imagination. Life is true-to-life among us, ad nauseam, and this may well summarize our condition. We have trained ourselves to graze on the very food we cannot digest.

We might theorize that the American mind has never been at ease with fiction, and that the average novel would have more readers if it was known to be free of it. Many of the novels we read, rather than merely admire, have the threat of libel about them, or they cunningly reveal what we have known all along to be the truth about our children. Boys who tell us all—from Huck Finn to Portnoy—we believe tell us the most about ourselves. The coinage of a language suitable to a boy is at the headwater of our literature. Portnoy merely reports to us further downstream, where there is more muck and pollution. Only the vernacular would prove to be equal to this awesome task. It's a remarkably fluent and melodious tongue, capable of astonishing moods and fancies, but its inexhaustible charm is to speak for what comes naturally. Its secret appeal and the heart of its thrall-dom is that we believe that ultimate freedoms cannot but give us ultimate truths, and that ultimate truths will prove to lie in four-letter words.

Mr. Mailer restates it in this fashion:

so Mailer never felt more like an American than when he was naturally obscene.

To be an American *is* rather something special, and one special thing about it is this matter of language. Is the ultimate vernacular a natural melodious flow of obscenities? Have we achieved it, or is it still lacking something in the way of melody? As Americans, we seem peculiarly addicted to pursuing freedom in one direction only—a descent into the rumpus-room wickedness of four-letter words. Down-ward paths to wisdom are always more photogenic, at their lower levels, than those directed upward, but the writer should not confuse evil doings in the subway, repulsive as they may be, with a view of the abyss. The terrors of Dante's Hell are technicolor snapshots compared to the depths living men have actually returned from. Perhaps only Americans feel such horrors can be exorcised by blasphemous remarks, and that for every terror there must be an equivalent obscenity. The reverse of covering up what is believed to be evil is to reveal it in the full light of day and judge it good. If the word is spoken aloud, if the dirty deed is done by daylight, if there is nothing known to men that is not known to all men, then the corrupting powers attributed to evil will disappear. The vernacular promises that glimpse of Eden before Eve looked upon herself and saw that she was naked, and to this extent it is the last sanctuary of the American dream.

In my judgment we are so affluent with writers of promise, with beginnings that look auspicious, that great beginnings may constitute a specifically American art form. The reverse of this coin is a predictable tendency to peter out. This is so common we are highly impressed by the occasional exception. Early achievement and premature recession may well be the linchpin in our cult of youth. If the middle-aging man were intellectually vital, how could we make a case for his early retirement? Nor is it unusual that the young writer, absorbed with the uniqueness of his own experience, will process it with more appeal and persuasion the *first* time than he will manage to do later. The books we love are about growing up more than about being grown. By its very nature the vernacular is sympathetic to first love, first triumph, and first rejections, but inclined to show wear in the repeat performances.

That he begins with a bang, often very large, then fades away to a repetitive whimper, can be traced to the writer's conviction that personal experience, preferably rugged, is his primary source material. When this lode of ore is depleted, he has shot his bolt. It is possible to postpone this crisis by pursuing life, as in a safari, bringing back for the stay-at-homes the loves and trophies of faraway places. But even this is at best a delaying tactic, based on the writer's virility and vigor. There is a place in it for the mature man —the big-game hunter with his female trophies—but there is no place for an old man whose life, if not his work, is behind him.

Readers of obituaries know the astonishment of learning of someone just deceased, long believed dead. Where had he or she *been*—other than out of our thoughts? We are agreeable to the premise that this writer was true to a life that is gone, but repelled by the thought that he might be true to the life we are living. We are young. And what we seek to be true to is youth. In both our theory and our practice we repudiate the nature of civilized life, the long life we can no longer avoid providing only the humiliations

62

of old age. Educated to anticipate their liquidation, the elderly are persuaded to go into exile on the fringe of golf courses, or in convalescent communes, or to take up residence in mobile homes, exposed to all the wonders they can no longer see clearly, or are forced into internment in slum hotels too small to have lobbies, from where they ambulate to cash the check that assures their social security.

That it is possible, among a free people, to prevail on its citizens to be outcasts is a matchless example of the brainwashing the vernacular makes plausible. No matter what the media, *they* get the message. Make way. What is currently spoken they hardly understand. What they do understand is explicit. The past is dead. The present and the future belong to the young. Not a word of this doctrine need be read for the citizens of the republic to accept it. It may or may not be true to law, but it is true-to-life. What life *is* can be instantly determined by taking a cross-cut slice of the vernacular, comparable to a bore at a buried ruin, which will reveal as much of the past as the present may find use for. The language that mirrors the life, the life that mirrors itself, surrounds the writer like the curved lens of a camera, persuading him to believe that what he sees is all there is. In this way we have become our own closed model of reality.

Free to write as he pleases, the writer is confronted with an open-air museum of ready-made materials, inexhaustible in their number, but curiously resistant to fresh combinations. Amazing how, with so much life to be true to, we end up with an overall impression of sameness.

In her review of the movie *Payday*, Pauline Kael reveals the virtues and the limitations of the true-to-life vision.

> . . . the movie keeps its distance at all times; we observe what the characters feel but we are never invited to feel with them. When we stay on the outside like this, there's no mystery. We don't sense other possibilities in the people; we never intuit what else they might have been, never feel anything larger in them than the life they are caught in. It's part of the picture's realistic integrity to show them for what they are, without sentimentality; yet to view stunted lives is not altogether satisfactory—as I think "Fat City" also demonstrated. This picture is much tougher minded, and it's up-to-date—it has none of the blurring, softening (and antiquing) effect of a tragic tone. I don't know *how* it would be possible to present this life as acridly and faithfully as "Payday" does and infuse into it the beauty of some redeeming illumination without falsifying and destroying it. But this realism is close to the realism of hard-boiled fiction; the astuteness is self-protective, and it prevents "Payday" from rising above craft.

The "beauty of some redeeming illumination" is very definitely not true-to-life, and it strains the rules of vernacular practice. Not the vernacular *itself*—the language will soar if the writer soars—but it is alien to common practice. You cannot both soar and keep your feet firmly on the ground.

In the mixed media of a few decades, Whitman's new and melodious tongue is the barbaric yawp of those who are not afraid of Virginia Woolf. A suburban brawl and a ghetto mugging are of one common language. In this commune low life and high life bed down together. All the words have been used, the wars have been covered, the concealed has been exposed, the unspoken spoken, yet we find that both the writer and the language are committed to more than they can deliver. What we are qualified to find—as distinct from what we pursue, perhaps the most tenacious of our fixed ideas—lies in the realm of the possible, a word that depresses the American eagle's intent to soar.

Where the vernacular dissolves an old distinction it provides a transparent but binding mucilage: if the discipline comes apart at the seams, the materials are reassembled for wider usage. The vernacular imperative might be defined as the painless dissolution of distinctions: that between fact and fiction, or art and non-art, or music and noise, or good and bad fiction. We have tests for food, for vitamins, for air and water, for gasoline, intelligence, seat belts, eyes, ears, and the blades of a razor, but we have no

65

test for good fiction. It is still what some people read who form the opinions that influence a few others. It is the strength and the frailty of good fiction that its persuasion is so fragilely based, yet proves to be indestructible.

Just Imagine

In a last Introduction to his plays, Yeats said, "As I altered my syntax I altered my intellect."

This is a mind-blowing statement, quite beyond our unaltered comprehension. It says simply that syntax shapes the mind, and it is syntax that does our thinking for us. If the words are rearranged, the workings of the mind are modified. Man is not free to think, as he believes: he is free to think along the lines syntax makes possible, as trains commute to those points where the rails are laid down. He is more of a prisoner of syntax than of sex.

This is the logic of the sentence, but it does not give us access to its full meaning. We must still imagine the many things inferred in what we do not fully comprehend. The reader senses a truth in the statement, but its full implications elude him. It is something new. His eyes glance from side to side, search the wall and the ceiling, for clues to its nature. In the presence of the bizarre we say, "Just imagine!" having no other resource to turn to. Conceivably, we might imagine that an altered syntax would alter man, and liberate him from his ruts of dead feeling, wrong thinking, and predictable behavior. Some intuition of this kind may have encouraged Shelley to speak of poets as legislators, altering men where they need to be altered, within themselves. However conceivable that might be, it has not taken place. Only a few writers a century tamper with syntax to the degree of alteration, and the results are not reassuring.

If we do not alter syntax, is the mind left unaltered? Do the rules that make lucidity possible unavoidably inhibit the imagination? To what extent does our need to explain an experience, in a clear and orderly manner, qualify or distort the actual experience? How many times, when we say, "What I mean to say is . . ." do we lose what was implicit in what we just said? Dostoevsky's Versilov makes this comment:

> If it happens that I try to explain an idea I believe in, it almost always happens that I cease to believe what I have explained.

This insight may apply to most minds of a creative nature. When the elusive truth appears to be cornered, the game loses interest.

In what measure does our need to possess what is new transform it, on the instant, into what is old? There is a loss—and the writer is the first to sense it—when he labors to explicitly clarify what is better left implicit. When we give up what is vague in order to be clear, we may have given up the motive for writing. Is there another way of saying:

> Still we know how Day the Dyer works, in dims and deeps and dusks and darks.

Joyce's example forced Beckett to further nuances and subtler alterations:

> . . . before the door that opens on my story, that would surprise me, if it opens, it will be I, it will be the silence, where I am, I don't know, I'll never know, in the silence you don't know, you must go on, I can't go on, I'll go on.

The lines were written by an Irishman, in French, then translated into English. Writing in French may have released Beckett from the predicament of writing English after Joyce. The syntax is different. In this release from the over-familiar, the apparently exhausted, and immersion into new resources, we may understand better than we did in the past the flowering of a talent like Conrad's. The new and strange language is part of new consciousness.

The writer accustomed to the technique of the "flashback" would find it hard to structure a novel without it. It is one of his tools. It is also one of his chains. The term itself is explicitly accurate: the backward look is a *flash* because the writer has no other way to get there. He must flash back, like a clever genie. He cannot, like the modern film maker, run his film, slow or fast, in reverse. It is quite impossible for the writer to actually retrace his steps. He must first flash "back," to a position of rest, then proceed forward in the usual manner. What was once a liberating technical innovation is now a somewhat tiresome cliché. Writer and reader both feel it. This early obsolescence of a technical "breakthrough" is one of the many side effects of the movies, where the film permits us to experience the reversal of time flow. This frees the film maker of many conventions that have served his purpose, but in still "thinking like a novelist" he has not grasped the new possibilities. It is the *novel,* not the film, that blocks the way. The convention of the forward-flowing story, a familiar narrative line, with flashbacks, blinds the film maker to the new horizons the film is technically prepared to explore. The *replay,* alone, alters the syntax of seeing what we think we see.

The movies are now part of a writer's raw material, and film technique has its place in the craft of fiction. The writer is relearning how to *see*, as the film maker is learning how to write for film. What the writer learns to see may influence him as much or more than what he reads.

Too much is still said of the writer, or the artist, ahead of his time. The fiction writer is not: the illusion is created by the number of his colleagues who lag behind it. It is the challenge to the writer to be of his time, as it is natural for his readers to lag just behind it. Kafka saw what was obvious, what was there to be seen, not something monstrous beyond the horizon. The others did not see it. Of all things, we are perhaps the most blind to what is obvious.

Kafka's gift was not modest, but he was right in constantly regretting its limitations. Like the princess in Hans Christian Andersen's "The Shadow," his malady was his talent—he saw things too clearly. This gift is the rarest of all writing talents, and comes to fruition without the strain of altering the syntax. To the one who sees what is obvious no special linguistic genius is necessary. There it is. What needs to be described calls for great simplicity. Gregor Samsa, who awakes to find he *is* an insect, is spared the conventional fictive torment of *thinking* he is one. How simple it is to see things clearly, no matter how complex the thought. In a world of increasing complexity and sophistication, the new in fiction will tend toward simplification, toward the obvious. To search and strain for it will only modify, at best, what is already old.

The native language so important to the writer becomes a predicament as writers exhaust it. Making it seeming-strange is one way of making it new. The bastion the French Academy has made of the French language would not have encouraged such an achievement as *Ulysses,* or survived *Finnegans Wake,* had it been conceivable. If a parallel deterrent had existed, France would not have been the cradle of modern painting. Manet, Monet, Cézanne, Picasso, the Fauves dispensed with the old and came up with the new. Had they been writers, not painters, they would not have succeeded. A frame can be enlarged, a painting hung upside down, objects distorted, dislocated, or dispensed with, but the structure of language is not so easily altered. The mainstream of the language has not been diverted by such a prodigy as Joyce. It appears to be the landscape, rather than the writer, that determines its direction. Language itself, in this context, is a seamless part of the fabric it is the purpose of language to examine.

The first thing to see, looking away over the water, was a kind of dull line—that was the woods on t'other side—you couldn't make nothing else out; then a pale place in the sky;

then more paleness, spreading around; then the river softened up, away off, and warn't black anymore, but grey; . . . and by and by you could see a streak on the water which you know by the look of the streak that there's a snag there in a swift current which breaks on it and makes that streak look that way; and you see the mist curl up off of the water, and the east reddens up, and the river, and you make out a log cabin in the edge of the woods, away on the bank on t'other side of the river, being a wood-yard, likely, and piled by them cheats so you can throw a dog through it anywheres. . . .

In this vernacular way Mark Twain conjures up a syntax suitable to his materials. It is not mind-shattering, but it is persuasive, and alters the syntax where it matters, in our feelings. Of special interest is the phrase "piled by them cheats so you can throw a dog through it anywheres." That is the writer's perennial problem: to write in such a manner that he penetrates the wall of clichés surrounding his subject.

Although worth prospecting, and to be borne in mind, mind-altering alterations of syntax provide the fiction writer with short term gains. His authority, no matter what the syntax, lies in the quality of life, of emotion, that his fiction arouses in the reader. Writers sometimes achieve this in spite of their syntax, as in the case of Dreiser. The language bends itself to his emotion. Lawrence is a writer where emotion and syntax seem to be of one substance. In the world of great fiction nothing is so strange as the commonplace, the familiar. The writer intuits this with certainty, but how does he realize this intuition?

In *The Brothers Karamazov*, Mitya has this dream:

> He was cold, it was early in November, and the snow was falling in big wet flakes, melting as soon as it touched the earth. . . . And as they drove in, there were peasant women drawn up along the road, a lot of women, a whole row, all thin and wan, with their faces a sort of brownish colour, especially one at the edge, a tall bony woman, who looked forty, but might have been only twenty, with a long thin face. And in her arms was a little baby crying. And her breasts seemed so dried up there was not a drop of milk in them. And the child cried and cried, and held out its little bare arms, with its little fists blue from cold.
>
> "Why are they crying? Why are they crying?" Mitya asked, as they dashed gaily by.
>
> "It's the babe," answered the driver, "the babe weeping."
>
> And Mitya was struck by his saying, in his peasant way, "the babe," and he liked the peasant's calling it "a babe." There seemed more pity in it.

Nothing is more common to the Russian scene than starving peasants and indifferent landlords. They are facts of life. The writer must make of this life what it failed to make of itself. In the peasant's way of calling the child "the babe," the commonplace is made uncommon, and Mitya is able to experience what is "constant in human sufferings." Pity is at the heart of Dostoevsky's torment, and never long out of his imagination. It also interested James Joyce, and he was at pains to give us this answer:

> Pity is the feeling which arrests the mind in the presence of whatsoever is grave and constant in human sufferings and unites it with the human sufferer.

The statement is lucid and appeals to the intellect, but the emotions of pity itself are not aroused. We turn to fiction for the experience that arouses and enlarges our capacity for pity, whether or not we ever come to understand what pity is.

We have a normal, familiar way of thinking, of feeling, and we use it in the familiar dilemmas of life. We are all subject, however, to fits of thinking, and seizures of feeling, that we both value and distrust. Flights we call them, not without reason. Flights of fancy, fevers of the imagination. We do not have them often enough to feel at ease with them, to rely on them, or to understand them. The ease, the reliance, and the understanding are talents we associate with the writer—one who feels as we do but has a way of realizing how he feels.

The writer too has a normal way of thinking and feeling, and he spends his normal life subject to it. It is a commonplace that writers are not as smart as the people in their books. They don't seem to learn much from what they are prepared to teach. This is because they live in the "real" world, as well as the one they retreat to after breakfast. The writer's not-so-normal thinking passes for lifelike in the context of his work, but he must be at pains not to deceive himself as to what is fiction, and what is life.

Both good and bad writers seek refuge behind the role of the writer as truth maker. Keats spoke of the truths of imagination. He went no further to define what he meant, out of respect, we may feel, for the subject. The imagination perceives and reveals, rather than observes. Either we see these lights glint on its surface, or we are blind to its nature. Since Coleridge, shelves sag with the weight of this discussion, but the reader must still grasp what is true, and perceive what imagination has revealed. Analysis of the words leaves us with analysis.

Highly "imaginary" writings—fantasies, fables, along with the new world of science fiction—are often strong in invention but weak in conception. They strain to be unusual, but it is the usual that puts the strain on the imagination. When the fiction writer turns to science fiction he will write one more good or bad novel, not one of a type. The distinction lies in the writer, not the genre. To be no more or less than a good novelist is the goal of the good science fiction writer. Science fiction, as a genre, is imaginary, rather than imaginative.

Periodically, in this world we have imagined, we must freshly conceive *who* we are, and *where* we are. In *A Portrait of the Artist As a Young Man,* we find this notation on the flyleaf of Stephen Dedalus's geography textbook.

Stephen Dedalus
Class of Elements
Clongowes Wood College
Sallins
County Kildare
Ireland
Europe
The World
The Universe

This is a picture of the facts appropriate to the occasion. Who Stephen was, and *where* he was. A limited but working model of reality. Soon enough, with the greatest deliberation, James Joyce would devote himself to more ambitious models. They have to be imagined. They have to be appropriate to the needs of the time. Small fry no longer ornament the flyleaves of their textbooks with such data. A sense of the aggregate, whether we like it or not, is displacing our sense of uniqueness. Men are in space, men are on the moon, the heart of one man pumps the blood of another, yet in individual men there has been a shrinkage in the capacity for wonder. We are dazzled by these awesome achievements, but our consciousness is not enlarged. These events simply add to the large sum of things we fail to understand.

Just as we imagined ourselves into this dilemma, we must imagine ourselves out of it. We either make to ourselves pictures of facts that are adequate, and life-enhancing, or they will prove to be inadequate and life-depressing. As of this moment in the twentieth century our predicament is an aggregate burden that only the individual imagination is empowered to relieve.

About Making It New

Pound may have been the first to give the thrust of doctrine to the American instinct to *make it new*. In so doing he gave official sanction to what came naturally to the natives. In the new world where so much had to be made, or remade, making it new was both an aptitude and a necessity. Tocqueville was the first to comment on what would prove to be built-in obsolescence.

I accost an American sailor, and inquire why the ships of his country are built so as to last but for a short time; he answers without hesitation, that the art of navigation is everyday making such progress, that the finest vessel would become almost useless if it lasted beyond a few years. In these words, which fell accidentally, and on a particular subject, from an uninstructed man, I recognize the general

79

and systematic idea upon which a great people direct all their concerns.

Aristocratic nations are naturally too apt to narrow the scope of human perfectibility; democratic nations, to expand it beyond reason.

". . . the general and systematic idea upon which a great people direct all their concerns." We make it new. We are ill at ease with the old. Educators who are eager to establish a "heritage" have had little success with the American public. Our attention is focused on the newest and latest, for which the earliest provides a measure of progress. The past itself is recreated, and made new, through such enterprises as Walt Disney Productions. The energy and passion we bring to "making it new" lie below the level of our discussion. It is our "business" when we say business is good. In the field of art, *making it new* is a highly respected obsession: newness—other qualities being absent—identifies the product as an art object.

To make it new—rather than make it good, or make it sound, or make it true—makes of the rejection of the past what there is of value in the creative act. The mystique of this act profoundly gratifies the artist who would like to have done with the ties that bind him, as well as the hand that fed him. To either make it new, or destroy it, brilliantly simplifies a very complicated matter. In its essence, it is an appeal to action, and generates rejection rather than creation. What is new this morning, tomorrow morning is already the past. The language itself excites the writer in its use and abuse of such a word as *new*. How much or how little did it have to do with such innovators as Eliot and Joyce, and such non-innovators as Thomas Mann. Mann is conceptually new (he is *contemporary*) without departing from traditional modes of fiction. The periodic resurgence of the avant-garde attests to the vitality of the imagination, but the deliberate pursuit of what is new proves to be a limiting performance, anticipating its own early obsolescence. If the talent is adequate, and the age provokes it, something new will appear as a matter of course; if not, the effort to make it new will result in little more than novelties. Originality comes as easily to the original writer as being a camel does to the camel. One Stein, one Joyce, one Rimbaud, one Beckett, to name a few, are more than enough for several generations.

At the end of the twenties, a renaissance period in contemporary literature, public fatigue with the crafty, well-wrought novel had much to do with the success of Thomas Wolfe's long and not so crafty but appealing and lyrical confessions. The Second World War provided the break that found the postwar younger writers reading Camus, Sartre, and Beckett, instead of Hemingway and Fitzgerald. During this period of absorbing new masters, the beat generation spoke up for the natives. The hippies put these complaints to music. As we approach the mid-seventies, my impression is that more good fiction is being written, and published, than at any time in our history, but there is no question that less and less of it is being read. The modern reader turns to nonfiction, as the novelist Mailer turned to current events. Both subscribe to the notion that the times are out of joint for fiction, a superstition that is old, rather than new, and has the grain of the American mind behind it. Thoreau did not read "novels," neither did Whitman or Twain, and they were apparently ignorant of William De Forest, the first to write about the war, the liberated female, and the freed slave.

The leading modern exponent of "making it new" is the French artist Marcel Duchamp. After painting his celebrated *Nude Descending a Staircase,* he turned from painting to create his series of Ready-Mades, of which the urinal exhibited in 1913 is the most famous. Although these conceptions anticipate Dada, they were not Dadaist in intent. Duchamp's highly theoretical mind sought for resolutions of esthetic problems as he later sought for the keys to chess. If he appeared to make light of Art, and like the Dadaists dispense with the concept, he took chess with the solemnity of a nuclear physicist. He is of esthetic interest for what he did—a series of original and audacious concepts—but he is famous for what he did not do: repeat himself. In the history of those who propose to make it new, Duchamp is one of the few to carry his ideas through to their conclusion. There is an end to making it new, and the artist either falls silent or he repeats himself.

The artist who paints, sculpts, constructs, or merely chooses has a wider repertory of options at his disposal than the writer who has only words. It is Duchamp's observation that "words are not merely a means of communication," as the collage has demonstrated, but for the reader of fiction interest languishes as novelty wears off.

Three original concepts provided Joyce with the labor of a lifetime, but the writer of the last twenty years is not inspired by his example. The author of "Rose is a rose is a rose" in her later years seemed more relaxed toward both roses and people. As a goal or principle for the writer of fiction, *making it new* is more pernicious than helpful, and eventually leads to frustration and silence. Newness has its place in the house of fiction—for much the same reason as the decorator but the windows face in all directions. So what is new? It is new enough if the craft is adequate to the inspiration. Fitzgerald credits Hemingway with this comment: "If Tom Wolfe ever learns to separate what he gets from books from what he gets from life, he will be an original writer."

That is not a small achievement for the modern writer, who cuts his teeth on books before he broods on experience, but it will serve him as a guide, and save him much strain, in his efforts to make it new. If he is a writer, and the writing is good, it is new enough.

About the Reading
of Fiction

Let's say the reader has bought the book, borrowed or thieved it, and has set himself down or sprawled on a bed to read it.

What makes him think he *can?*

Reading is a mystifying ceremony: like prayer, it is best done with the lips, in silence. Look closely at a reader. His absorption is intense. It is hard to share a room with a companion reading. The nonreader is excluded. He can only experience the absence of his companion. Where is he off to? By what cunning can an arrangement of words engage the reader in a distant experience? Or even one close at hand, a journey within himself?

What is it he reads?

I see the book on the table.

Is that all? What could be plainer? A simple declarative sentence. It can be found in all language primers. But if we put this simple statement in a fictive context . . .

"What do you see?" asked Popkov, without turning to look.
Bergdahl replied, "I see the book on the table."

. . . the simple statement is now complex, and we are at a window in the house of fiction. Even the name Popkov adds a flavor. Perhaps Bergdahl is a spy in from the cold. Seeing the book has a meaning that is subtle and elusive. Popkov's simple question is menacing and ambiguous. When he turns to fiction, the nonfiction reader is disturbed by the way things are not what they seem. To be other than they seem, indeed, is almost one of the rules of modern fiction. Why is that? It is one of the disturbing facts of modern life. There is a fiction for all sorts of readers, but no realm of fantasy is as strange as the everyday fabric of life. In the past half century much of the best of modern fiction often seems intent on confusing the reader. To say one thing and to mean another—or not to trouble to say it, to imply it, or leave it unsaid.

Mother died today. Or, maybe, yesterday; I can't be sure. The telegram from the Home says: YOUR MOTHER PASSED AWAY, FUNERAL TOMORROW. DEEP SYMPATHY. Which leaves the matter doubtful; it could have been yesterday.

What is the speaker's intent? What is the author's intent? Here is a character who does not seem to know, or much care, if his mother died today, or yesterday. What sort of fellow is he? Is he a soulless, shallow cad, or pretty much, in some ways, like the reader? We get a hint of that if we go on reading, if we want to know.

These opening lines of Camus's *The Stranger* reveal Meursault's confused state to the reader, and something of the reader's similar state to himself. This will be neither apparent, nor poignant, to the reader who has not learned to read *fiction*. Nothing is explained, or will be explained: what is shown must be perceived, apprehended. The reader's pleasure is often in proportion to what is left unsaid, or ambiguously hinted. To read such fiction well is to grasp some of the skills involved in its creation. As in music, the writer calls for this response, playing on the sensibility of the reader. In a way that lies below the level of discussion, where the writer and the reader share the same subconscious, paradox and ambiguity give the aspect of truth to our constantly changing impression of the facts. In these shifting crosslights where nothing is clear, they reassure us that we see things, however poorly, as well as we can. We have lost our assurance that we see them pretty much as they are.

Many readers of sophisticated nonfiction are perplexed

by relatively simple novels. What are they about? Why do readers and critics have such contrary opinions? Most readers of Erich Segal's *Love Story* wept—why did a few laugh? One might know these readers personally, and listen with sympathy to their opinions. Is the reader to admit that the same novel leads one person to tears, another to snickering? Nonfiction doesn't do that, or seldom. The reader's perplexity may actually seem to amuse him: you may even see him smile.

This dilemma is not uncommon when a work of fiction attracts large numbers of occasional fiction readers. Like an amateur lover, or gambler, this reader is seldom prepared for what lies in store for him. He takes words and signals at their face value. He weeps when the occasion calls for weeping. He is furious and humiliated to learn that someone "clever with the cards" has taken him in. The cuckolded reader of novels has the smoldering wrath of a woman scorned.

With *Love Story* the problem is simple. It both abuses and uses the clichés of fiction. These clichés then abuse and use the inexperienced and vulnerable reader. The serious problems of fiction begin with the reader who is not inexperienced. He may well be a reader of considerable cultivation, having read the "great" novels in college. When this reader is assured a modern novel is "great," he feels obliged to buy it and make the effort to read it. Curiously, it is the "great" new novel that resembles the old ones which provides him with the keenest disappointments. Something big out of Russia awakens his desire for a parallel fictive experience. These are the novels, well promoted, and heavily sold, that are soon found partially read in secondhand bookstores. Even the inexperienced reader is soon aware that this does not feed him where he hungers. Caught between boredom and humiliation, he reads reviews rather than novels. He echoes the fashionable cliché that the novel, if not dead, is declining. If one he hasn't read turns up in a movie, he will go to the movie and be reassured. He has heard, and accepted the cliché, that movies are the art form of our time, their goodness or their badness explained to him by the reviewer.

What has happened to the reader that fiction, through its own efforts, might have averted? It has never had the power, in spite of some boasting, to shape the reader to its own image. It administers rather than transforms, and it mirrors rather than changes. In profoundly mirroring the age, it has lost the bewildered and harassed reader. He wants escape. It is the intent of fiction to persuade him, often against his will, to be engaged. Considering the nature of this task, and the reader's increasing reluctance to read, the modern novelist achieves a small but crucial triumph: for what it is worth he is conscious, and holds consciousness an ultimate worth.

What is *modern* in fiction is also what proves to be difficult. This difficulty can be traced in the changes involving the first-person narrator, a reliable source, in the traditional novel, for the author's authority. There are other voices, sometimes heard in a chorus, but the voice of "I" was usually unquestioned. The price paid for this was high, limiting the author to one window in the house of fiction. The advantages were that the reader believed what he was told. The mystique of the "I" is implicit in Whitman's

I was there, I saw, I suffered. . . .

From Huck Finn to Alex Portnoy, the "I" is used by adolescents to assure us they are telling it like it is—indeed, speaking *personally;* how could they do otherwise? In these confessions the presence of the author was acknowledged, but the reader assumed it would not be exploited. Of course, Twain was in Huck Finn: of course, Salinger was in Holden Caulfield. That could not be helped: that was *why* it was fiction, and gave it such appeal. But the reader never questioned where he stood, or that he failed to grasp the author's complex purpose. The ambiguity, nevertheless, was always there, and waited on the circumstance to be encouraged.

Thomas Mann is covertly in Aschenbach, as Joyce is in both Stephen Dedalus and Bloom. To the experienced fiction reader this skillful overlapping results in a pleasurable enhancement and richness. Nor does the author's presence seriously hamper the occasional fiction reader. The story line is clear: both author and reader know where they stand.

The deliberate use of this overlapping is the modern contribution. What could better mirror, in so many ways, our indistinct impression of identity? Our uncertainty as to who it is who dramatizes the flux and relativity of our sensations? Italo Svevo was one of the first to see the "I" gain in interest for being unreliable. Henry James gave it a try in *The Turn of the Screw,* and provided critics with a century of research. What *did* he intend? It defies resolution, and interests many readers who are bored by good fiction. By the time Camus had in mind *The Fall,* the unreliable narrator was a mode of fiction. That consummate rogue of our time, Clamence, baits the reader with his frequent likeness to the author. Was that Camus's purpose? Or was it one of the risks, and the enticements, in using the first-person form of narration? There are things one cannot help. One says, "I . . . I . . . I . . ." until one is the "I." In this confusion of identities we are often at a loss to say who it is that speaks. After all, *whose* Fall is it? The reader is one of the first to recognize his own likeness. But Camus's suggestion that Clamence is a portrait "of the aggregate vices of a whole generation" on reflection is not satisfactory, a ploy that seems intended to lead the reader off the scent.

To puzzle out the nature of this aggregate portrait requires a scholar's interest and analysis: Clamence himself becomes increasingly unsubstantial. In one short novel we find on exhibit what is "difficult" in contemporary fiction: intellectual audacity, the sportive play of irony, paradox, and ambiguity, these elements agreeable to the sophisticated sense of our orderly-disorderly times. The unreliable "I" of Clamence's narration is ideally suited to the author's purpose, but leaves something to be desired by the reader who crouches with the book in a train seat, his impending Fall more personal than aggregate.

The ideal reader of fiction is hard to determine, as teachers of literature have long known. We have no true way of appraising what a reader gets from a book. Good fiction, especially, would seem to be at the mercy of the reader's vulnerability. If he is *en garde* he is off target. He must be open to fiction at precisely those points where he has been closed to life. To ask all of that is too much, of course, and readers and writers are both losers. To the extent a work of fiction can mean so much, it is dismaying to find it can mean very little. The novel and the reader wait on the chance that will bring them together, like lovers. No two readers, if the fiction is good, can be said to have read the same novel. Non-fiction can be appraised in regard to its content, and sensibly discussed in regard to its message, but the good story or the great novel is possessed, if at all, on individual levels that are unique. The work of fiction that unlocks the soul of one reader is, by its nature, closed to many others. Readers of Hemingway are seldom readers of D. H. Lawrence. These two writers alone contradict the notion that a single reality waits to be captured. Lawrence, Hemingway, Joyce, Stein, and Faulkner are writers of fiction with contrasting, on occasion contradicting, impressions of the facts. Thomas Mann put it this way in one of the dreams of Joseph:

> But lo, the world hath many centers, one for each created being, and about each one it lieth in its own circle.

This is an insightful and appealing metaphor, but it no longer speaks to what disturbs us. There are too many centers, and the numberless circles are in constant agitation. What we seek is a whole in which these centers will be at rest.

About the Reader

It is a tradition among writers, like honor among thieves, that they get their novels from a publisher, free; from the author, autographed; from a friend, borrowed; purchased secondhand, or sampled while browsing in a bookstore. A few pages are enough to assure one writer about the new fiction of another. It will be something he looks forward to reading, or is grateful he has been spared. Only on rare occasions does this circumstance find its resolution in a bookstore. To *buy,* quite simply, is a departure from principle. The origins of this tradition may lie in the mists of time, but the root it has taken in America can be clearly traced to the Great Depression, when there was time to read fiction but a lack of money to buy it. In those days most good novels published were remaindered a year or two later. I myself bought hundreds. My trips to town, any big town, were largely remainder-buying orgies. One could rely on the best of contemporary fiction for thirty-nine cents.

The purchase of a novel at the publisher's price gave rise, in the writer, to guilt feelings. To the question "Where did you get that book?" any answer would do but that he had bought it, unless at cut rate. My first actual purchase of a contemporary novel in a bookstore was Katherine Anne Porter's *Pale Horse, Pale Rider,* in Waterbury, Connecticut, and my fear to wear it out prematurely led me to put off reading it for several days, then I read it with marginal notations to make sure I missed nothing. American writers *do* read fiction, but it is a point of principle not to buy it in a bookstore at the going price. Writers, that is, provide their own reader predicament.

They are joined in this compact by teachers of English and other academes who have a taste for fiction. Some will prove to have been pioneers of the True Depression, with short- or long-term careers in the Writers' Project, well trained both to value books and to read them, but to buy only *nonfiction.* Reference books they were called. Necessary to a scholar in his work.

Among the first to be taught what libraries were for were the children of such writers and teachers. There was the college library, then the public library, as well as the private libraries of more affluent colleagues. Right up through the Depression the good fiction of the twenties could be found on the shelves that framed the fireplace. Not all of it, of course, but enough to cultivate the taste for more of it. In the late thirties these books gathered dust and the only new titles were nonfiction, such as John Gunther's reports on the outside-inside world. At the end of the Second War the paperback revolution seemed to offer the solution to both writers and readers. The young, in particular, were eager to read anything that was new. They wanted the latest. They wanted the now, the relevant, the existential. The youth rebellions and the paperback book combined to form a new reading public, with the college campus as its center. Paperbacks were available everywhere, but quality nonfiction and the best of modern fiction were to be found in the bins of the campus bookstore and the pockets of its students. In this manner the first distinction was made between the two emerging reading publics: the one to which quality would have an appeal, and a continuing, although modest sale; and the one in which supply and demand would follow the familiar merchandising patterns. To a degree that is measurable, *quality* in fiction is an encumbrance to the best seller. The quality appraisal has its place on the campus—the quantitative in the bookstore, where the reader of fiction remembers the title but forgets the author, or remembers it wrong. In this circuitous way the failure of the writer, of the academic reader, to exercise his influence over the bookstore counter has left the "general reading public" to the mercy of the sales pitches and promotional budgets. If the book is "selling," the reader can find and buy it. If not, he can place an order for it, and over the weeks spent waiting for it to arrive observe the way his impulse to read it has faded: by the time it arrives it is no longer the book he might have read.

If writers alone, who now number in the thousands, would buy the novels they have every intention of reading, the publishing of good hardback fiction would be on a sensible commercial basis. Here is one crucial predicament of fiction that writers of fiction have the power to alter. One fault of the paperback revolution is to have spread the word that books should be *cheap*. This complaint, the expense of books, has it loudest support among the chronic nonbuyers, who find in something so sensible as money the root cause of their nonbuying status. For those who value books lightly they should be cheap, and they are. Those who value them dearly—would two seats at a first-run movie fit that description?—might reappraise their priorities while still faced with the possibilities of a choice. If all novels are to be cheap, the choice will be made by somebody else.

About the Fly in the
Reader's Ointment

A student of the modern novel recently asked me—off the cuff, and writer to writer—if I didn't think the fly in one of my books was a symbolic cliché. The Midwest setting of this novel buzzed with trapped flies, and so did the book. They were buzzing flies when they came to my mind, and they were trapped flies when I put them on the page. They belonged to the scene I was painting as the screen door belonged to the porch, the way it banged when it slammed, and the view through the fly-spotted window. Flies, dead and alive, were among the first inhabitants. That they might also prove to be symbols was not my proper business. Symbols are not what happens on the page, at the writer's bidding, but what happens, unbidden, to the reader. When the writing is good everything is symbolic, but symbolic writing is seldom good. Symbol hunting is the hobby of the student too jaded or too "smart" to read.

The overtrained symbol-haunted reader will not accept the fly for what it is to both the author and the book. An actual trapped fly. Such a reader wants to talk about flies as symbols, not about the flies that buzz in the mind like a magneto, crawl about on greasy and napping faces, swim and drown in warm lemonade, are swallowed down in dippers of well water, strew the floor beneath the window like popcorn, stick as if glued to lumpy light cords, and are born to turn up trapped between the rattling window and the cracked yellow blind. Before it is made into a plastic object to be embalmed in cocktail ice cubes, the fly is first, last, and always an outraged, mindless, maddening, unforgettable fly. From intimate experience with many such flies symbols will still emerge.

What loss is there to the reader if the fly is not reborn as a symbol? The pleasure in this awareness is part of knowledgeable reading. It is one of many craft recognitions that subtly bind the writer and the reader. Each one brings a pleasurable shock, a reassurance of familiar vibrations.

This experience parallels the delight we take in the moth or butterfly in a state of nature, and the same creature in a state of preservation identified as a *tiger swallowtail*. The first impression is so ineluctable, so elusive, as to evade categorization: it belongs to the mystique of experience as the *tiger swallowtail* belongs to knowledge. Obviously, the curious mind craves both, but literature is not the field for the data seeker. A different level of consciousness seems to be engaged in the student who is studying *The Sound and the Fury* and the reader, however naïve, who has his mind's eye on the sparrow. For this experience the student of fiction must wait until the scaffolding of craft has been removed, and no longer obstructs his appreciation.

Literature has been a matter of taste for so long that a taste for literature is taken for granted. It is assumed, that is, that where we have books there will also be readers. That there is something to do with a book *besides* read it has opened new horizons. Here are a few of them:

Pre-reading—giving a quick, searching scrutiny to the material to see what it is about and estimate its interest.

Phrase-reading—learning to read in phrases, not words. Taking wider "visual bites" as your eye moves across a line of type.

Skipping—selectively jumping over large sections of material after pre-reading has sized it up.

These new skills, among other things, mark the end of the traditional relationship between writing and reading, between reader and writer. The writer must still learn to write (it is assumed) but the reader need only learn to read faster and faster. Apparatus to speed up slow readers is now distributed by book clubs, on the safe assumption that club books are piling up behind slow readers. Quick, searching scrutiny persuades most of such readers to skip club books.

There is nothing we can do with the melancholy fact that numberless readers of novels actually dislike fiction, and search the season's crop of novels for nonfiction that is feebly disguised. Lovers of music know that many listeners to music are actually tone deaf, or wish they were at concerts, and connoisseurs of painting number among their friends color-blind enthusiasts who are mad about art. This is how things are, and the writer, the painter, and the composer make peace with this fact as they do with the weather. It cannot be denied that strange sounds have the power to soothe the savage breast.

Igor Stravinsky once made these comments:

> . . . but don't forget that *Petrushka, The Firebird*, and *Le Sacre du Printemps* have already survived a half century of destructive popularity, whereas, for example, Schoenberg's five orchestral pieces, and Webern's six, have been protected by fifty years of neglect.

Protected by neglect? Implicit in this comment is a chilling appraisal of the modern production and consumption of the arts. In accepting the accuracy of this appraisal, I question its relevance to the writer of fiction. Orchestral pieces may or may not age, like a good wine, but if played they require listening. The novel requires reading. Either the reader takes the time to read what is written, or what is written will suffer from more than neglect. Rather than facing outward, to such readers as there are, the writer will understandably turn inward, a more destructive twist of the screw than a few seasons of popularity. If he seeks an adversary, none other is so vulnerable as himself.

The Ideal, Built-in,
Nonexistent Reader

One custom has it that the writer is basically writing for himself. In this light he is his own ideal reader, and there is, on occasion, some truth in it. Left entirely to themselves, however, writers might start but they would seldom finish a novel. Alone in the mountain cabin, or under the palms on an island, a diary would soon suffice:

> Today saw smoke of steamer on horizon.
> Later it rained. Too windy for fishing.

Like so many highly personal facts, they don't add up to much as fiction. In the fullness of time the writer senses the emergence of another reader. If he can trust his impressions, the book he has written has within its pages its own sought-for reader. This reader is a seamless part of the novel, a palpable yet invisible part of the fiction. He appears to the writer at those moments of indecision when he casts about in his mind for reassurance. The voice he then hears is not his own, nor is it the voice of "truth," or some cunning of his ego: it is itself part and parcel of the fiction's intent to be as fully achieved as the writer can make it. He knows more, as he writes, than he knew at the outset. It is the "conscious" part of his expanding sense of craft. He is creating, as the work progresses, what he needs to know. It is sometimes easy (in this situation) for the writer to persuade himself that he is flirting with vaguely extrasensory perceptions, but these perceptions, where they prove to exist, are merely the function of his talent. The way he shapes a line, the way he fashions a scene, the way he is implicit or explicit, bears in mind the reader he might be himself, if he were not a writer, and the fiction he would like to read if he were not obliged to write it.

What we choose to call "style" is the presence in the fiction of the power to choose and mold its reader. The sought-for reader, in this view, is the first of the fictions the writer must create, and it is why, for such a writer, the opening lines of a work are so important. There is the voice that seeks to hold one reader enthralled, turn another away. From a vast surround of indifferent readers *this* reader has been shaped to be the true believer, or so the writer hopes.

To this end he both bends and shapes his talent. In this knowledge the writer is empowered to write with more assurance than he otherwise might, and the reader is vested with more than his customary talents to read. Writer and reader are part of a single imaginative act. Most writers would like to mount such readers as trophies, forgetting, in their need, that they are fictions. To these ideal, built-in, nonexistent readers they dedicate their books.

About the Campus City

A HAVEN FOR WRITERS, READERS, AND GOOD FICTION

Some years ago I felt the predicament of the novel was of one piece with the decline of the reader. More than a decade of teaching has persuaded me, however, that readers for fiction are not disappearing. The campus reader ranges in age from sixteen to sixty (a few to eighty) and all have had more experience of life than literature. Some have been to war, others look forward to revolution, and they read novels for answers to these real-life problems. There are more sophisticated ways to read, but this is one way to challenge the writer. In a characteristic bypass of history, these readers want light on the immediate present. The modern novelist who dramatized such issues—Mailer and Vonnegut, Beckett and Camus—found that he had a new subculture reading public. The taste of the campus reader seldom parallels the taste of the "general public," or makes its influence felt on the hardback trade edition of novels. It is almost exclusively a paperback phenomenon. A separate public, of separate and conflicting tastes, took root on the campus in the late forties and is now firmly entrenched. Just as the sophisticated reader considers himself detached from the marketing scene of best sellers, the campus reader has neither knowledge of nor interest in the promotional world of bookstore hardbacks. He has his *own* store. He has his *own* books. He has his own standards of assessment and appraisal. The campus is a subculture free of the pressures, the persuasions, the hokum, and the confusion of the marketplace. Both cliques and cults exist, but the writer is evaluated as a writer. The campus reader reads the book, as well as the bookstore copy of *The New York Review.*

If there is a loss of glamour in this new scene for the writer—many of these readers consider themselves *writers* —there is a gain for the work of fiction. Writers and novels are seen to be a real part of the world's action. That public that receives its best sellers in the mail, and its opinions from reviewers and pundits, is less absurd than largely unknown. It is part of a culture that the campus reader assumes to be dead. The hardback book itself, priced from six dollars to fifteen dollars, is a symbol that distinguishes life styles; the abused, cheaply held, and thrown away paperback is to that extent like a worn-out garment, part of the lived past. The respect is for its substance, its shared experience, and seldom if ever for the book as an object. That taste will come later, if at all, and its loss is not crucial.

The epidemic of thievery common to the campus, involving books, school supplies and equipment, knives, forks, and salt cellars from the cafeteria, derives from the tribal assumption that these are not objects so much as services. (It also derives from common thievery.) In taking the *book* for granted, as part of their diet, they have diminished one of its enduring values, but their attitude toward its content makes many of them excellent readers. They want to know. They think there is something to be learned from fiction. They will continue to read out of motives measurably less involved with grades and status, or part of an experience limited to their "growing up."

To what extent should the writer's craft of fiction be of interest or concern to the average reader? Both the writer and the reader are in general agreement that what one needs to read a novel lies within the novel, but what one gets out of it lies with the reader. One important detail is overlooked. The writing of fiction requires the writer's concentration for weeks, months, and on occasion years: the reading of fiction is believed to be a matter of intermittent concentration for five or six hours. Dynamic Institute readers are said to scan an average novel in less than an hour. The writer of fiction puts into his novel such powers as he has, talent as he has, and experience as he has: the reader budgets him so many hours of his time. In magazines of the thirties, the time required to read a story was posted to attract or warn off the reader. The commuter could adjust his fiction to the length of his ride.

To give some semblance of sense to this practice, it is assumed that the writer's craft of fiction is to achieve effortless reading. The reader lies back, preferably in a hammock, and the author does all the work. Fiction for "summer reading" was surely crafted with such a reader in mind. With the turn of the century, however, the emphasis of good writers has been on the writing, rather than the reading. What the writer learned to write, the interested reader would learn to read. Much of this reading was done by writers anxious to share their enthusiasm with the public. Pound and Ford Madox Ford established canons of taste to which both writers and readers strained to adhere. Without this almost boundless respect for the craft of writing, much that was written would have seemed absurd. The obscurities of *The*

Waste Land, or Joyce's *Ulysses,* were the hallmarks of breeding and distinction. A poem or a novel that was not "difficult" was better ignored. No volume so short as *The Waste Land* has ever received such long and respectful attention, and the published fragments of *Finnegans Wake* were collected by readers of religious commitment, fragments of the true cross. This period "between the wars" will baffle the younger writers who give more attention to life than literature and merits the interest of the critic who would like to know how such demanding writers ever gained and held a public. Good Reading for the Millions, a paperback slogan, has displaced the difficult reading for the few. The reader who is unaware how profoundly novels differ, and why one is intricate, another transparent-seeming, is leaving the better part of such fiction as he reads unread. These distinctions are present, through talent and effort, and the reader is challenged to possess them. To judge for himself what is good, not merely what pleases, liberates the reader from a cloud of unknowing: he is free at last to read novels, rather than reviews. With much reading and a little patience he will blaze his own trail through the jungle, here and there finding a clearing where he meets the writer on his own ground.

In one way or another the modern writer seeks to involve the reader in the "writing experience" and persuade him that this experience is the one he seeks. The *writing,* not the story, is at the heart of the matter, and where the reader must look for its elusive meaning. So it is little wonder that such fiction now produces more writers than readers, leaving the reading to those better classified as amateurs.

About the Decline of
Fiction—If There Is One

According to a recent survey, three out of five Frenchmen have not read a book since childhood. No distinction is made between good books and bad. They have not read a book. Reading books is no longer a necessity of life. For literate Frenchmen this constituted a major cultural shock. It strikes at the heart of the mystique of *la gloire de la France*. In an effort to combat this crisis, the French government proposed to give each newly married couple five volumes of French classics. Perhaps only in France could agreement be reached on what these volumes should be. It is of interest that poetry was excluded from the list because its effect was often depressing.

If Frenchmen do not read books, what can be said of Americans? The decline of the reader is one of the facts the writer of novels must acknowledge. The decline of the novel is a superstition agreeable to both critics and readers. Statements about the state of the novel are baseless. Neither a single critic, nor a group of critics, can be described as familiar with the vast fabric of fiction. Or is it easier to say the novel is declining than deal with thousands of new novels yearly? Is there more to this current disenchantment with fiction than our sense of frustration with the age in general, in particular with *words?* Words and more words, a ceaseless flood of words, and we observe that they change nothing. That it is their very nature to mock and delude us. That the art of fiction, at its most crafty, is to say one thing and mean another. The scale of the dilemma has led to the agreement that only a handful of writers "matter." Only matter to whom? To critics, so there is a basis for critical discussion. To have a discussion it is a help if the participants have read the same books. So the critics who matter read the fiction that matters, and discuss among themselves what matters.

It has always been so, but it is new to have so much fiction that *doesn't* matter. Reviewers read some of it. Nobody buys it. The author sends a copy to the writers who matter. If *they* read it, maybe he too will matter. It's surely worth a try. He reads the critics to see if he might be mentioned among the "younger writers who should be encouraged," whose novel, *Fuse,* stood head if not shoulders above the seasonal flood of trash, whose author, on the strength of this work, was not in the usual rut.

The word *rut* appears so often in critical discussion one might think it was a new form of fiction. The French novelist and critic Robbe-Grillet comments:

> Hence it will be the specialists in the novel (novelists, or critics, or over-assiduous readers) who have the hardest time dragging themselves out of its rut.

What rut is the novel in? In Robbe-Grillet's opinion, the early writers of fiction—Madame de La Fayette, Balzac, Flaubert, etc.—learned how to write a particular novel from which the writers of today have not departed, hence the rut. The word *rut* is well chosen to describe this predicament. Ruts are the result of heavy, often brutal, traffic over limited lines of communication. That is explicitly true of the novel. Modern traffic in the novel, in America alone, runs to tens of thousands of volumes yearly. The limited channels for this traffic, what constitutes a bona-fide, recognizable novel, means that the ruts grow deeper and deeper.

As a writer of novels, Robbe-Grillet also knows that ruts make novels possible. Equally important, they make and sustain readers. Without the ruts, without the flow of fiction that is good, bad, and indifferent, the novel would be the private pastime of a small pack of obsessed writers. To give up the rut is to give up what makes the novel possible.

This can be seen in the current disorder of what not long ago was known as painting and sculpture. They are now free of "ruts." They are also free of all means to consider, to compare, or to comprehend them. This confusion will very likely come to an end when it has traveled full circle, and the original ruts are newly established. A retrospective of the "painting" of Norman Rockwell, recently held in San Francisco, may give some clue to the nature of the rut some rut lovers would like to reestablish.

The novel has been spared this particular confusion, good solid ruts, even in times of change, being a sign of its health. The novel, like the novelist, needs ruts to keep it from wandering for years in the bush. As a novelist Robbe-Grillet surely knows that, but as a reader of novels he is also bored with it. That is understandable. So am I. Most writers, and the majority of readers, would like to see a few novels new as all get-out. But how likely, or desirable, is this? Novels arc about people. People arc not made new yearly. Over several centuries good novels have proved how *alike* they are, rather than how different. *Finnegans Wake* begins

riverun, past Eve and Adam's, from swerve of shore to bend of bay, brings us by a commodius vicus of recirculation back to Howth Castle and Environs.

That is the durable, unchanging role of the novel, "commodius vicus of recirculation."

Do we need more explicitly new novels than we have? Robbe-Grillet writes them, Madame Sarraute writes them, Beckett, Barth, and Barthelme write them, just to cite a few lying on the counter. Novels that are *modern* but not so explicit, that rattle along in the ruts and are often lost in them, represent what is "new" in the novel without the need of putting down new tracks. D. H. Lawrence is such a writer, Thomas Mann is such a writer, Fitzgerald, Hemingway, and Faulkner are such writers. They write most of the great fiction. Their example sustains the ruts of fiction and assures their extension into the future. Such remarkable departures as *Finnegans Wake* have not diverted the course of the novel, nor palpably transformed the human imagination. It's still the same old story. The writer's burden is to keep it fresh.

But if the rut is so good, if it keeps the channels open, if it makes the writing of good and bad fiction possible, why do we justifiably complain about it?

The accumulation of novels over several centuries, and the backlog of literature this provides, results in the fact that most writers derive their inspiration, and not a little of their substance, from what they read rather than what they experience at first hand. In America, the book of life was still open during the first half of the twentieth century, and the firsthand reports on this life gave the American novel a power and a freshness the European novel understandably lacked. The Europeans were more *bookish* writers, erudite and self-aware, their efforts largely determined by the novel's "situation," compared with the grass-roots renascence of Twain, Crane, Dreiser, Anderson, Fitzgerald, and Hemingway. (Henry James, in the European tradition, was predictably literary in his orientation.) Fresh talents were largely the result of fresh life, and as the life lost its freshness the talents diminished, and proved to be in ruts of their own making. If we look around us, this is what we see in America. The European writer, with little fresh to exploit, his culture and his milieu unchanged for centuries, had to rely on his talent and his imagination to make new what was already old. T. S. Eliot, as a matter of both observation and intuition, assumed that the only way out was to become European and use the resources of history as raw material. Eliot's "new" poetry is an inspired recycling of poetry that he considered important to the maintenance of culture. To his temperament, the flood of new raw material threatened to make art and literature impossible. He saw the intricate imaginings of Joyce as

a way of controlling, of ordering, of giving a shape and a

significance to the immense panorama of futility and anarchy which is contemporary history. . . .

For Eliot the problem was that of tradition and the individual talent: what was new in the talent would reveal itself as traditional, as orthodox. The lack of this "orthodoxy" led him to read D. H. Lawrence out of the High Church of Art.

To this emerging disorder, discernible in the twenties, we yearly add hundreds of novels that escape critical comment and defy pigeonholing, but are of necessity obliged to maneuver in the old ruts. Understandably, the critic views this with alarm, and the reader with indifference and growing confusion. Is the novel declining? Are a few *in*clining? Is it dissolving into a hybrid of fiction-nonfiction? To talk about this problem—not to resolve it, but to be merely able to discuss it—the critic chooses a handful of representative writers he assumes are read by representative critics: Bellow, Barth, Roth, Nabokov, so forth. These are all good and accomplished writers, but they do not provide a purview of the novel, or a clue to the state of fiction. The production of fiction is now so vast that no sensible purview is possible. The younger writers, with few exceptions, are all remarkably schooled in the *modern* novel, but understandably limited in terms of experience. Their premature schooling in the craft of fiction results in their fiction resembling other fiction, and the increasing vernacular texture of our lives heightens this impression of sameness. (I have discussed this elsewhere.) The paradox is that the craft of fiction, among the young writers, has seldom if ever been on so high a level, and it is largely because of this that it gives the reader the impression it is *like* the old, and indeed it is. In this wise the writer learns to write, and pays suitable homage to his master. To make a novelist, however, it takes not only talent, it takes time.

In the flood of modern fiction, much of it good, it also takes luck and winnowing, since readers for the best are hard to come by. No critic or group of critics, no reader or group of readers, has a respectable way of estimating the vast amount of fiction now being written, and until a respectable means is found, all talk about the state of the novel is fiction, and most of it bad. The small sampling of new novels I happen to read is not only promising, but frequently achieved, and will favorably compare with what was being written, day in and day out, during the great periods, time having winnowed down those periods to four or five names that are still familiar. Fifty thousand or more novels were published in the twenties. How many are now remembered? To compare a moment of the immediate present with the carefully sifted remains of the past is to parade ignorance as knowledge and add further confusion to the issue. We do not know what the *state* of the novel is, but we know that it is alive.

Is there more to the current disenchantment with the novel than our sense of frustration with the age in general? There is not, so long as the novel faithfully mirrors that frustration. If we look to fiction for *how things are,* what do we expect? Everything is wrong. Is there something we look to fiction to change? We are back where the American dream first came in—great expectations and premature dis-illusion—which finds its expression in ceaseless bitching or causes that elude all possible resolution: worldwide hunger, or immediate and lasting peace.

Predictably, we strike out at what we have at hand, and readers strike out at what they are reading. There is too great a choice, there is too much that remains unread. This single fact provides the irritant that leads to sweeping gen-eralizations. It is easier to damn the novel entire than try to winnow out what we are seeking. Nor does it lie within the powers of fiction to ease or cure our psychic discomforts. Books are vulnerable, we leave them on train seats, they do not give off rays or springs of lifesaving water, they require sounding, they require the risk of being out of one's depth. They are powerless. It is the reader alone who can turn them on.

For something less than a century, American writers could strip-mine the raw materials of American experience. These materials were everywhere for the taking. Numberless writers still rake around for ore in these slag heaps. Both the writer and the reader (in his boredom) sense a parallel between our vast consumption of natural resources and the writer's narrowing resources of fiction. For a few that is good. It has brought them back to resources of the imagination. For the thousands less gifted it means that their fiction will continue to bore the reader of fiction. He has read the books the writer has read and the one he plans to write. Both writers and readers congregate in cities where the illusion of complexity is convincing, and many levels of life, as at Troy, can be seen in operation. The life goes on: the lives are familiar and disposable. Parodies of city life now flooding TV testify to these burned-over fictive areas. The inexhaustible richness of the rich and poor prove to be exhausted in a few seasons. Given the appetite of the American public, and the means to bait, whet, or gratify it, what aspect of American life could long survive a "rediscovery"? Nothing on this earth, beneath it, or around it, will long prove inexhaustible.

It is the games *people* play, of all the games there are, that preoccupy the fiction writer. However advisable it might be for a change—a view of life in which *people* are not at the center—both the reader and the writer of fiction are committed to people. The occasional exceptions will merely reinforce the rule. Changes in fiction have always been desirable, and have come about through changes in people, through changes in craft. When great resources of people are available, as was true in this country for the past century, the writer felt himself handicapped in having only one life to deal with them. Varieties of people were numberless and inexhaustible. Changes in both life and fiction soon narrowed these vast resources. As varieties of life impressed the readers in the twenties, similarities impress him in the seventies. This fictive impression of American life derives as much from literature as from life, and from life that recently derived from literature. The documentaries on TV reassure us that real wars and those in novels are similar. The high level of devices of reproduction, tapes, films, etc., combined with the full spectrum of the vernacular, leave little to the imagination in the assembly of a "real-life" portrait. Paradoxically, it is this fact that deprives the "real-life" image of interest. We know it, we see it, we hear it, and we try to absorb and reject it daily. This particular function of fiction is no longer necessary. It is what we failed to see, to hear, and to know that once more must absorb the writer. All of this must be imagined—intuitively grasped and cunningly crafted into language. We don't lack such fiction, but it is usually lost in the flood of the prevailing product. The serviceable vernacular deceives many readers into believing they grasp the fiction in reading the language. What the writer gains through this common language may prove to be the writer's loss. He looks, in the vernacular, more available than he is. William Gass's *Omensetter's Luck* appears to be a model exercise in the language that everybody reads and too many write. The uninitiated reader will soon enough give up, with serious misgivings about the novel and the author. However much it sounded like the usual thing, it proved to be something else.

This dilemma will not soon be resolved, since we have spent half a century creating it, but the first step will be taken when we see it clearly. Gabriel García Márquez is a contemporary writer, born in Colombia, South America, who writes in Spanish. He lives in the modern world, but he has not been shaped by American fiction. In *One Hundred Years of Solitude* he has written a novel that he hopes is true to the imagination. Other truths would impress him as inferior. Or he might well ask, what other truths are there? His mind and his book have roots that are deeper than the recent history of modern fiction. It is a quixotic book, blending, at any moment, the real and the fanciful into his own fabulous recounting of the history of one family. If he had been persuaded to be true-to-life in the prevailing manner of contemporary fiction, he could have given us little more than what we have in overabundance.

In our *resemblance* to fiction, most of it bad, to its specifically true-to-life dimensions, we fail to see the most obvious elements in it, furnishings that we habitually refer to as the true-to-life. As I write these comments, the TV features a twelve-part serial of "An American Family," an enterprise on the scale of a Hollywood production, involving seven months of filming and approximately two million dollars.

Did anybody ask *why?* No question need be asked if we have the assurance it is true-to-life. Real people, real problems, and real good cameras getting it down. Both the producer and the family knew this would prove to be of interest. *That,* above all, is what it is to be an American. Not knowing actually *why* they were of interest, they were open to a project that might help explain it. Then *they* would see, then we *all* would see, what might be of interest in an American family. The natural self-esteem, the natural self-infatuation that needs no more than itself to feed on is the only fact of interest the program has thus far revealed. Each member of this decent, well-favored family is on an ego trip, and the painful vacuity of these trips is all that provides the report with its subject. Only human beings so culturally conditioned that they are blind to what they are seeing could sit through one hour of this program without a shock of horrifying recognition. This has not as yet occurred to members of the family. The revelation of the program is considerable in terms of the bathos of the lives presented, and the regrettable fact that one member of the family is at work on a book dealing with this "experience." The predicament of our lives and the predicament of our fiction are seamlessly joined in that intention. Both are captive in an illusion that we describe as the true-to-life.

For some centuries now the Western ego has been culturally force-fed, like the geese whose liver is prized by gourmets, until its original and organic function has become a malfunction. The ego trip is not a universal human disorder but a culturally nourished derangement, so omnipresent in our ego-oriented culture that we accept it as perfectly normal, a sure sign of life. The person who recovers from this dis-ease may well find the peace that once passeth understanding, and the writer who recovers from this obsession may find that he perceives what was once concealed, and to speak of veils being removed from his eyes is to speak of his recovery from an ego inflation.

I write these words, and stop to ponder what I have said. What have I managed to suggest to the reader who does not already feel as I do, that the ego trip is at long last reaching the end of its run? Currently it is in space, recording data, or taking snapshots of our threatened planet, or in laboratories, greedy for knowledge, or in the seats of both the low and the mighty, and day and night it feeds intravenously the monster that stalks toward Bethlehem to be born. It is where the reader sits, where the writer sits, where the poet and the genius burn both ends of the candle, but if it makes for good fiction, I reassure myself, it makes for life.

About Voice

OR, THE WRITER REVEALED IN
SPITE OF HIMSELF

Voice is the presence in the style of what is most personal to the writer. Through voice, the writer is invisibly omnipresent. It might be likened to the palette of a painter, or the characteristic sound of a composer. The reader says, "Ah, Joyce!"; the observer, "Ah, Matisse!"; the listener, "Ah, Stravinsky!" The signature is apparent in the fragment. These elements of craft are open to analysis, but analysis will not explain why they charm us. To perceive the writer in his many disguises is one of the great pleasures of reading. Behind his masks we detect his own ineffable voice.

All good writers have a voice, but it plays a special role in the craft of fiction, where it reassures the reader that he is getting more than information. The words play on the ear, have a taste on the palate, linger and malinger in the mind.

. . . the childman weary, the manchild in the womb.

What is that—besides Joyce? Voice is what we perceive when we follow the writer from book to book, ". . . the ineluctable modality of the audible." As the voice becomes more evident, more assured, it is less subject to fluctuations, to what is unpredictable. Where the writer once possessed the voice, the voice slowly possesses the writer. And where this voice is mannered, as in Hemingway, we note that it exerts a power over the writing. How to achieve a voice and not become its victim is one of the modern writer's concerns. What is original in his voice will prove to lie beyond the writer's choice or control.

In *Three Lives* the voice of Gertrude Stein is both provocative and deceptively simple. The apparently simple proves to be complex. Events are subordinated to consciousness.

She wondered, often, how she could go on living when she was so blue.

The language is musical but without strain, as if it came as naturally as conversation. And that point is crucial. To flow as smoothly as talk, if talk were capable of flowing smoothly. Of another writer Stein said, "He has a syrup, but it doesn't pour." Words that flow or fail to flow, words that are like honey, treacle, or molasses. Stein's feel for the vernacular was matchless, and left its imprint on both Anderson and Hemingway. Sherwood Anderson's voice is so pronounced—the artless storyteller conscious of his story— that he is open to parody.

> You can see for yourself how the old man, who had spent all of his life writing and was filled with words, should write hundreds of pages concerning this matter.

Hemingway was quick to seize on this voice and try to mock it in *The Torrents of Spring*. His own voice is so marked, however, we cannot detect the voice he hoped to ridicule. *The Torrents of Spring* is a parody of Hemingway by Hemingway.

As we read him in translation, Thomas Mann's voice is leisurely, impersonal, and reassuring. We feel in good hands. He is free to step from the wings of his fiction and clarify a point, or ask a leading question.

Who shall unriddle the puzzle of the artist's nature?

Implicit in this storyteller's stance is the assumption that there is either time enough for what needs to be said, or no time at all.

For, after all, what more pitiable sight is there than life led astray by art?

This is the author, speaking to us as directly as the words on the page will allow, but they lie at peace with the others in the complex mosaic of *Death in Venice*.

There is little of this artful "distance" in Lawrence, where we are seldom free of the sound of his breathing. The manner in which Ursula and Gudrun, Birkin and Gerald, are completely realized and original creations, yet each permeated by the voice of Lawrence, is one of the mysteries of talent and craft that make the study of fiction gratifying. Lawrence is often intrusive, the reader can hear him gnashing his teeth and audibly hissing, but this static is not the voice of Lawrence that matters. Speaking of Gudrun, he says:

> Once inside the house of her soul, and there was a pungent atmosphere of corrosion, an inflamed darkness of sensation, and a vivid, subtle critical consciousness, that saw the world distorted, horrific.

The searing voice of Lawrence burns through this sentence like a fire through brush, a crackling flame without smoke.

Scott Fitzgerald is familiar, casual, low-keyed—before we know we are listening, he has our rapt attention.

In my younger and more vulnerable years my father gave me some advice I've been turning over in my mind ever since.

"Whenever you feel like criticizing anyone," he told me, "just remember that all the people in this world haven't had the advantages that you've had."

That is the voice of Fitzgerald, and its timbre is a unique blend of sentiment and money. The sentiment lends it the grace that Hemingway attributed to courage.

Another writer had this mastery of voice when speaking in the first person. Ford Madox Ford begins *The Good Soldier* with this sentence:

This is the saddest story I have ever heard.

The powers and the hazards of the first-person voice are epitomized in this sentence. Are we to believe what we are told? Or is it meant to be questioned? How do we distinguish, with assurance, between the "I" of the narrator and that of the author? Is the ambivalence deliberate or unconscious? Ford's novel anticipates, by more than thirty years, the delights the modern reader finds in the ambiguous and the mockingly ironic.

Faced with the same narrative problems, almost forty years later, Camus is as abrupt as a chance encounter. Only later, when we put down *The Fall*, will we ponder the illusive meaning of what we have read.

The modern writer's voice is invariably crafty, but it will seldom be highly literary, as in the past. The rise and triumph of the vernacular established different standards of judgment: to appear to be artless, rather than artful—to seem to be doing no more than what comes naturally. When the novel is narrated in the first person, by a character who bears some likeness to the author, the deliberate and artful control of voice is subject to subterranean divagations, which the author may openly exploit or covertly find gratifying. Hemingway speaks Hemingway in "The Snows of Kilimanjaro," and Clamence speaks for Camus in *The Fall*. On this level, the presence of the writer in the fiction exceeds the controls normally active, and he reveals and confesses more than he intended, perhaps more than he knows.

Third-person narration, or the rhetorical "we"—a familiar and durable authorial disguise—provides the writer with the distance necessary to detect his own intrusions and over-exposures. The "I" voice is at once the most available and the most difficult to master. It is happiest when speaking for an adolescent, where naïveté is prized and candor is appreciated. In a story of his boyhood, Isaac Babel writes:

> As a boy I was given to lying. It was all due to reading.
> My imagination was always on fire. I read in class, during

132

recess, on the way home, at night—under the dinner table, hidden by the folds of cloth that reached down to the floor.

Nothing ambiguous here. So it must have been, just as he describes it, and the authority derives from the first person, the "I" who tells it like it is.

Other voices are equally revealing. Céline writes:

> The greatest defeat, in anything, is to forget, and above all to forget what it is that has smashed you. . . .

And Virginia Woolf:

> Often she found herself sitting and looking, sitting and looking, with her work in her hands, until she became the thing she looked at—

And Camus:

> "Oh young woman, throw yourself into the water again so that I may a second time have the chance of saving both of us!"

In these fragments each writer's fictive voice is discernible. It may be highly personal, or highly impersonal, but in either case it provides the writer with the maximum means of expression. Through voice he learns what he feels, and hears what he thinks.

Throughout this discussion about fiction many voices have whispered at the ear of the reader. They are all eager to snare, to entertain, to instruct, and on occasion to transform him. So there are risks involved. On good fiction should be printed a suitable caution from the Surgeon General. Take heed: the virus may prove contagious, and the effects may defy treatment.

The creations of fiction walk the streets of our cities, pursue love in the suburbs, go up and down in the world, or meditate in the forests, having taken the clues to their natures from a skirmish with good and bad fiction. We are of imagination all compact, whether we read fiction or not. Rather than become lucid, a perilous condition, we might aspire to becoming more human, an estate that the great talents of fiction have long given their fullest attention. Before becoming something else, conceivably worse, fiction invites us to consider what it is we are.

The fiction writer is not so confined as the lion, nor is he as free as the eagle or the falcon, but he is now in a position to see that the corridor of man's history is narrow, and that men stand at both ends of it, blocking the light. We yearn to be different, but we prefer to be as we are. The new fiction we envision, and all await, may appear to us fresh as the egg of a sea bird, or it may so resemble the old we will be at a loss to observe the difference. This difference will be a matter of our enlarged, or our diminished, consciousness. But in the writer's reluctance to leave the familiar he is under the spell of his own invention, and gives his support to the conceit that all things exist for man's pleasure and adornment. Not to be at the heart of the matter—is that too much? The first fiction to light up man's early darkness concerned itself with this problem. What one needed first was an imaginary garden, with real live toads. Then an Adam, an Eve, and the complications apparent in the serpent. So far so good—but now we risk a crucial step. Adam and Eve, having erred, are cast out of the garden. The moral intent is obvious, but it might have been a tactical error. Man as a separate creature, man going it alone, man forming in packs against dissimilar creatures, and predictably soon forming in packs against other men. From the perspective his brief history provides, we are nearing the end of a remarkable performance. For all its variety, and occasional promise, it has been a one-man show. Man has been its measure, and his measure is the planet's predicament. How long will it be before the writers of fiction wake from this obsession and look about them? The view from space, if it could be assimilated, if its mind-stretching message could be admitted, might divert men's eyes from the mirror he holds to himself. A palpable shrinkage of his ego, a measurable enlargement of his imagination, and he might well look about him and see what has been concealed since he was cast out of Eden. But he had better hurry, or little of it will remain.

At the beginning of this century the writer believed in the potency of his craft to alter human nature, and improve human life. As we enter the last quarter of the century he is less ambitious. The sounds that too many writers hear in the night is that of their nails scratching the bottom of the barrel. Both writer and reader are weary of these excavations in the cellar of the house of fiction, while a fresh breeze is stirring the curtains at the upper windows.

"Come to the window," says the voice to the reader, revealing the writer in spite of himself.

A Reader's Sampler

The query "What should I read?" identifies those readers of fiction who have stopped reading good fiction. They would like to read novels if they could only find novels they could read and like. The amount of good fiction waiting to be read is one of the facts the reader may find depressing. There is too much. It defeats the reader's impulse to make a start.

In contrast to this reader is the one who has read the 100 Great Novels and the numberless small ones. He has the lists. As he read the books he checked them off. What he seeks is a novel worth his trouble that he hasn't read. Such a reader is a trophy hunter, and his walls are hung with his triumphs. Great experience, on safari, has trained such readers to bag their books without bloodshed or misadventure. In answer to the question what they should read, they reply, "I've read that."

The titles I have assembled provide a sampler of twentieth-century fiction. There should be something old, and something new, for readers of various tastes and persuasions. The titles have in common the stamp of good writing they will share with knowledgeable readers. Here and there, meeting at random, a book and its reader make connection, and for the life of that bond there is more life to be lived, more life to be cherished, as well as to be lost. The losses are real, but great fiction assures us imaginary gains.

SISTER CARRIE *1907*
Theodore Dreiser

Suppressed on its publication in 1900, Dreiser's first novel was not available in bookstores until seven years later. This fact provides a measure of the changes "realism" introduced into twentieth century fiction. How do we chart the course between *Sister Carrie* and *Portnoy's Complaint*?

In the modern craft sweepstakes Dreiser is a bungler, a writer sometimes so bad his rhetoric seems campy, but his heavy hand does not long conceal his knowledge of people and what it is that corrupts them. He knows about life, and that is what the fiction writer should know the most about. Speaking of Carrie he observes:

> All that evening she sat alone in the front room looking out upon the street, where the lights were reflected on the wet pavements, thinking. She had enough imagination to be moody.

The awkward phrasing and perception are characteristic of Dreiser. Carrie and Hurstwood are people so close to me that I am ill at ease when the writer fumbles, and profoundly moved when he scores his points. The modern reader will experience, through Sister Carrie, a view of life that is outmoded but haunting, since Dreiser's people—almost against his will—get satisfaction from the world that deceives and destroys them. An instinct to be true to his feelings saves Dreiser's characters from his didactic intentions. A sense of emerging life, emerging *American* life, with its poignant and destructive blend of dream and reality, is as present in Dreiser as in Fitzgerald, but the potion is not so saturated. Dreiser too is an American dreamer brooding on the dark fields of the republic, but he is not so self-obsessed or so self-indulgent. Carrie and Hurstwood, Jennie Gerhardt and Cowperwood, mean more to Dreiser than reflections of himself. They exist: they are more than phantoms of his desires and frustrations. The text for his sermons could once be seen on the maps that decorated the lobbies of railroad stations, where the lines of force, from all corners of the nation, converged on the hog butchering city of Chicago. New York is another country. Our literature is at its best when the ties that bind prove impossible to cut.

This introduction to twentieth-century fiction was appropriately written by an American in exile. The "new" American language, anticipated by Whitman, was used with unexampled mastery. Stein admitted to the influence of Flaubert's *Trois Contes,* in particular *A Simple Heart,* but her tales owe their power to her use of the vernacular. The revelations seem so artless that early readers thought the author naïve, lacking literary instruction. Through alterations of syntax and skillful repetitions, she transformed a language shaped to the needs of men to one responsive to the feelings of women.

Remember, Mrs. Lehntman was the romance in Anna's life.

In the tale of *Melanctha* Stein achieves a remarkable portrait of women in love, a decade before Lawrence. In the manner of the modern painters she admired and collected, whose work supplied her with parallels and insights, she then turned to new experiments rather than building on what she had achieved. This made her famous, but deprived her of readers. Great innovators—and she is one of the greatest—make their impact on a few writers, who, in turn, will charm the public. *Three Lives* is the first fiction that seems entirely free of the obsessions that dominate the male-written novel: it's all a matter of feeling, an utterly womanly rendering of the complex simple heart.

THE NOTEBOOKS OF MALTE LAURIDS BRIGGE *1910*
Rainer Maria Rilke

When James said, "Try to be one on whom nothing is lost," Rilke might have been his ideal listener. This work was written in Paris, and tests Rilke's youthful powers to record the last nuances of his impressions.

> So, then people do come here in order to live; I would sooner have thought one died here. I have been out. I saw: hospitals. I saw a man who swayed and sank to the ground. People gathered round him, so I was spared the rest.

Who would think to compare Rilke with Céline, but for a moment they share the same Paris. Céline would have been a boy of about fifteen. "Travel is a good thing," he wrote later. "It stimulates the imagination. Everything else is a snare and a delusion. Our own journey is entirely imaginative. Therein lies its strength."

Rilke lacks the rage and stamina of Céline to rub his nose (and the reader's) in what disgusts him. But he is like Céline in his eye for suffering, and his gift to intuit even more than he sees. A larger part of *The Notebooks* is concerned with

Rilke's imaginary journey into his past, where he is free to mingle truth, poetry, and fantasy, but these passages do not grip the reader as do the views from Rilke's window on the real world.

> In the street below there is the following composition: a small wheelbarrow, pushed by a woman; on the front of it, a hand organ, length-wise. Behind that, crossways, a baby-basket in which a very small child is standing on firm legs, happy in its bonnet, refusing to be made to sit. From time to time the woman turns the handle of the organ. At that the small child stands up again, stamping in its basket, and a little girl in a green Sunday dress dances and beats a tambourine up toward the windows.

DEATH IN VENICE *1912*
Thomas Mann

Readers turned off by the symbol-haunted modern novel are often at ease with the fiction of Thomas Mann. He's in no great hurry. He explains things as he goes along. In a narrative tone that recalls the past, he reveals what we find disturbing in the present. He is at once old and new, and his gift is the mingling of the mythic and the present moment. The vast scale and erudition of Mann's major novels should not discourage new readers from his shorter fiction. For all his range, Mann's special talent is the poetry and insight revealed in the gesture, and the expressive posture. This speaks to him of the ideal and the universal manifested in the involuntary movement. The lad Tadziu, in *Death in Venice*, is one of these archetypical figures, the consummation of ideal beauty.

He wore an English sailor suit, with quilted sleeves that narrowed around the delicate wrists of his long and slender though still childish hands. And this suit, with its breast-knot, lacings, and embroideries, lent the slight figure something "rich and strange," a spoilt, exquisite air. The observer saw him in half profile, with one foot in its black

145

patent leather advanced, one elbow resting on the arm of his basket-chair, the cheek nestled into the closed hand in a pose of easy grace. . . .

Such is the figure that lures Aschenbach from his summit of composure through various levels of decline to his death in Venice.

The reader is free, as he must be in fiction, to draw conclusions from his reading appropriate to his own experience. Full possession of a novel is not found in its critical appraisal and explication, but in the fresh levels of re-experience that occur with repeated readings.

THE DEAD from *Dubliners 1914*
James Joyce

In exile, in Trieste, Joyce fell to brooding on that fen of Irish bogs, Dublin. Distance almost lent it enchantment. He recollected the scene with affection. Exile also led him to dwell on the ceaseless commingling of the living and the dead, one of his lifetime preoccupations. "The Dead" is at once a prodigal's lament and a troubled lover's message of reconciliation. For once his portraits have a soft edge, and the romantic juices of his nature are allowed to surface. From Trieste he had written to his wife: "Why is it that words like these seem to me so dull and cold? Is it because there is no word tender enough to be your name?" This line he inserted into his story, as he would soon insert all that life offered into the vast mosaics of his fiction. Young men are drawn to write of older men, as they are lured by a life they have not yet experienced, and "The Dead" is Joyce's anticipation of the losses an older Joyce must suffer. In this tale there is so little of the formidable technician, the detached, satirical, clinical observer, that readers familiar with Joyce's reputation may wonder if this is the same author.

WINESBURG, OHIO *1919*
Sherwood Anderson

The reader who has just read Lawrence, and Gertrude Stein, will relax with this writer shaped by their achievements. Anderson has the same preoccupations, but less demonic energy and what we call talent. In these tales of the emerging American conscience he sometimes gropes for more than he grasps. In a few, however, he weaves a spell that will captivate many younger writers. Hemingway felt it, and grew to resent it. We know how he panicked at the thought of competition. It made him a bully, quick to turn on those to whom he owed the most. In *Winesburg* there are moments of tenderness and revelation quite beyond the reach of Hemingway's talent. On the shelf with the best writers of the century Anderson is soft and without contours, a ballad singer with a sly smile who hints at more than he actually says. His world is dimly lit, shadow-dappled by trees that line dirt roads and open out onto fields, the air fragrant with the smell of grass that the sunlight seldom gets to. Twilight: a mood of vagrant reflection and nostalgia. A habitude of yearning, of adolescent frustration, and of dreams touched with madness. In the dark fields of Fitzgerald's republic this was a familiar state of being, and Anderson was its poet.

THE GREAT GATSBY *1925*
F. Scott Fitzgerald

Now that Fitzgerald is back in fashion, many readers will have read this novel. Lucky for them. Perhaps they can now read it again. Few books come into this world with the perfection of a bird's egg, and this is one of them. The major strands of American life and sentiment come together in a manner that seems artless, and in this small book achieve a flawless appraisal. The big dreams are here, trailing their neuroses across the landscape like fireworks. Sentiment is so powerfully saturated it stands up in the lights like substance. Through its draperies we see the green light burning on Daisy's dock. For the writer of fiction, the miracle lies in the instant transformation of life into fiction: the achievement of a tone that gave Fitzgerald the distance to grasp in fiction what escaped him in life. He is himself the ticking bomb in this virginal American landscape, and as his imagination saw it deflowered he prepared himself for the wake. Fitzgerald "believed in the green light, the orgastic future that year by year recedes before us," and while this timeless pursuit remains he will speak to both those who look forward to it and those it has deceived.

WOMEN IN LOVE *1921*
D. H. Lawrence

There is no one comparable to Lawrence, and this novel alone is a match for his talents, his torments, and his passions. No writer of the century is more open to life, and speaks for all life, against man the great polluter. In this matter alone the young should find him prophetic. Lawrence's fury so heats his nerves that he gives off sparks, and they seem to crackle. Between extremes he is a blur of movement, at rest only at the top of a swing. He gives too much. He demands too much. His characters are possessed by primal forces, and exhaust the startled, word-throttled reader.

This was Hermione Roddice, a friend of the Criches. Now she came along, with her head held up, balancing an enormous flat hat of pale yellow velvet, on which were streaks of ostrich feathers, natural and grey. She drifted forward as if scarcely conscious, her long blanched face lifted up, not to see the world. She was rich. She wore a dress of silky, frail velvet, of pale yellow colour, and she carried a lot of small rose-coloured cyclamens. Her shoes and stockings were of brownish grey, like the feathers on her hat, her hair was heavy, she drifted along with a peculiar fixity of the hips, a strange unwilling motion. She was impressive, in her lovely pale-yellow and brownish-rose, yet macabre, something repulsive. People were silent when she passed, impressed, roused, wanting to jeer, yet for some reason silenced. Her long, pale face, that she carried lifted up, somewhat in the Rossetti fashion, seemed almost drugged, as if a strange mass of thoughts coiled in the darkness within her, and she was never allowed to escape.

That is Lawrence. No one matches him in candor that is free of vulgarity. No reader can say he is as fully conscious as he might have been while ignoring Lawrence. I might go on and on about *Women in Love*, but the reader need not feel intimidated. It's only a book. He can pick it up and he can put it down.

THE CONFESSIONS OF ZENO *1923*
Italo Svevo

One of the germinal encounters in modern literary history took place in Trieste in 1907. Ettore Schmitz, a Jew of German-Italian parentage, and successful manager of a paint company, took lessons in English from James Joyce, an Irishman in exile. The two men became friends. Joyce showed Schmitz some of his own work in progress, and Schmitz revealed that he, too, hoped to be a great writer, and had published two "unsuccessful" novels. From Schmitz Joyce acquired the Jewish lore so essential to *Ulysses*, and from Schmitz's wife, Livia, the name and the long golden tresses of Anna Livia Plurabelle. It was from Joyce that Schmitz, alias Italo Svevo, first heard that he was a "much neglected writer," encouragement that made it possible for him to begin and complete *The Confessions of Zeno*.

Svevo is a master of tone—intimate, gently ironic, his candor civilized and self-mocking—an ideal instrument to record the life and torments of a man who had turned to psychoanalysis to cure his addiction to cigarettes. The modern reader will be interested to note the long history of this malaise.

2 February, 1886. To-day I finish my law studies and take up chemistry. Last cigarette!!

A later entry in his diary reads—

4:30 A.M. My father died. L. C.

For whomever it may interest, he explains to the reader, the last two letters stand for "last cigarette." Svevo is compared to many writers, but no other modern writer com mingles the strange elements of his nature with the time and place essential to their flowering.

Alert to trivia as the record of human folly, Svevo is one of the first to feel a new dread in the old abuses. The reader is not prepared for the book's conclusion, a cry of havoc that discounts Zeno's tone of ironic amusement and boredom. In these lines Svevo is like an actor who comes before the footlights as the curtain falls, removes his mask of ironic detachment, and blurts the truth.

When all the poison gases are exhausted, a man, made like all other men of flesh and blood, will in the quiet of his room invent an explosive of such potency that all the explosives in existence will seem like harmless toys beside it. And another man, made in his image and in the image

155

of all the rest, but a little weaker than them, will steal that explosive and crawl to the centre of the earth with it, and place it just where he calculates it would have the maximum effect. There will be a tremendous explosion, but no one will hear it and the earth will return to its nebulous state and go wandering through the sky, free at last from parasites and disease.

And last cigarettes.

IN OUR TIME *1924*
Ernest Hemingway

The captivity of Hemingway's style still sends men on safaris, gives tone to war and murder, comforts the loser, and draws trout from the streams of our imagination. The young read him to find confirmation of what they already know. He was the first to grasp that overlarge expectations give rise to bad losers, and that grace under pressure is the bullfighter's option, not the bull's. *In Our Time,* a small packet of stories and sketches, casts the shadows that measure Hemingway's full life. Young writers will see the old master learning his trade, knee deep in the currents of the Big Two- Hearted River. At once contagious and indefinable is the tone achieved by the author's style.

> A GIRL IN CHICAGO—*Tell us about the French women, Hank. What are they like?*
> BILL SMITH—*How old are the French women, Hank?*

The candor and self-mockery of this tone were new, and those who heard it for the first time lost their interest in other music. It had its beginning along the Big Two-Hearted

River, and as of now there is still no end to it. He shaped so many of us to his ends, the time was partly of his own making—not the best of times, no: but not the worst of times either. Readers of Hemingway could judge this for themselves, having been there.

RED CAVALRY *1926*
Isaac Babel

It is curious that Americans, bred to violence, in a culture increasingly obsessed with violence, would have heard so little of Isaac Babel. *Red Cavalry* and Hemingway's *In Our Time* were both written in the early twenties, and owed their quality to the violence of war. Although Babel is drawn to war, his fascination is less romantic than that of Hemingway and Crane. He does not point up violence for its shock value, but observes how impartially the light glints on it as it does on other elements in the scene. Babel's comic genius, revealed in his tales of Benya Krik and other Moldavanka gangsters, displays, to my taste, a more original gift than his sketches of the Cossacks. He is not *tough:* he does not go to war to observe his grace under pressure. His war stories are glimpses of horror in which all the parts contribute to the dazzle. This links him to Crane rather than Hemingway, and to literature rather than life, in his search for clues for the perfect rendering of the writer's detached involvement. This artfulness, which leaves the reader without the safe shelter of moral judgment, may be more than enough to turn off the larger public. There is no moral outrage. Babel's mocking irony and elegant tone merely grate on the reader's discomfort. The reader receives no assurance as to how he should feel, and what he should think.

RED LEAVES *1930*
William Faulkner

The spectacle of human folly gives rise in Faulkner, as it did in Twain, to outbursts of mythic humor. The frontier provides the landscape for this humor, which is often at the heart of a wilderness. Twain had his Territory Ahead, Faulkner his tribe of fabulous Indians. In the story "Red Leaves," this is the world of Issetibbeha, Ikkemotubbe, Log in the Creek, Herman Basket's daughter, and that white man David Hoggenbeck who taught the steamboat where to walk. The outpost is peopled by blacks and Indians, and is a place where violence, the white man's noise, is kept at bay. It is here that Faulkner gives full rein to his humor, and finds no suitable occasion for his rage. The landscape itself, parklike and serene, is suffused with a light softer than moonglow. The man called Doom had his name from de l'Homme, and hence Doom. As a young man he had made a journey to Paris, where he met the Chevalier Soeur Blonde de Vitry. They lived in a house reconstructed of a dismantled steamboat.

What had been the saloon of the steamboat was now a shell, rotting slowly; the polished mahogany, the carving glinting momentarily and fading through the mold in figures cabalistic and profound; the gutted windows were like cataracted eyes. It contained a few sacks of seed or grain, and the fore part of the running gear of a barouche, to the axle of which two C-springs rusted in graceful curves, supporting nothing. In one corner a fox cub ran steadily and soundlessly up and down a willow cage; three scrawny game-cocks moved in the dust, and the place was pocked and marked with their dried droppings.

There is nothing to compare with this world, and it preserves an attic corner of Faulkner's vision of the good life, before the white man corrupts it.

JOURNEY TO THE END OF THE NIGHT *1932*
Louis-Ferdinand Céline

At the close of *Death in the Afternoon* Hemingway writes:

> No. It is not enough of a book, but still there were a few things to be said. There were a few practical things to be said.

The author is boasting, and seeks in this manner to solicit praise. In his own opinion he had written well, and reduced the sum of what remained to be said. He had discussed such things as death, matadors, and bulls, and relieved himself of quotable opinions on Spanish whores and contemporary writers. Very serious stuff. Writing at the same time, a French doctor, Céline, published a volume entitled *Voyage au Bout de la Nuit.* In it he observes:

> We shall never be at peace until everything has been said, once and for all time; then there will be silence and one will no longer be afraid of being silent. It will be all right then.

What Céline had to say occupied a lower level than Hemingway's style and machismo would permit him to descend to, or even admit to. Céline is the first to become lucid: looking about him, he sees what is obvious. Both the absurd and what is fashionable in black humor have their roots in his rage at human folly, the grain of his style a remarkable blend of realism and hallucination.

> That's what moving about, travelling, is; it's this inexorable glimpse of existence as it really is during those few lucid hours, so exceptional in the span of human time, when you are leaving the customs of the last country behind you and the other new ones have not got their hold on you.

The traveller who enters Céline's country does so at his own peril. If we are not yet at peace, it is not due to what he left unsaid.

THE DEATH OF THE HEART *1938*
Elizabeth Bowen

"Innocence," the author tells us, and it is the subject of this novel, "so constantly finds itself in a false position that inwardly innocent people learn to be disingenuous. Finding no language in which to speak in their own terms, they resign themselves to being translated imperfectly. They exist alone. . . . The system of our affections is too corrupt for them. They are bound to blunder, then to be told they cheat. In love, the sweetness and violence they have to offer involves a thousand betrayals for the less innocent. Incurable strangers to the world, they never cease to exact a heroic happiness. . . . The innocent are so few that two of them seldom meet—when they do meet, their victims lie strewn all around."

Portia and Eddie, who meet in this novel, chart the death of the heart in its early and late stages. At twenty-three the heart of Eddie is failing, but he seeks to recover its health in his love and concern for Portia, who is sixteen. A large company of worldlings surround them, in various stages of adult heartlessness and corruption. The author's knowledge of the heart in these first afflictions, and its downward path to wisdom, is unmatched.

American adolescents "spill the beans" in the full and complicit knowledge that someone will clean them up. Their grasp of both innocence and corruption is shallow compared to Portia's, whose heart is so full under siege it is her very nature that is under attack.

This beautiful novel is at once contemporary and traditional. What is new is a matter of the author's intuition and her wisdom of life. Loss of innocence, indeed, would be less poignant in unfamiliar surroundings. Miss Bowen is not so effective with her adults—who are obliged to be accomplices in this crime—but no writer is more at home in the hearts and minds of adolescents.

LET US NOW PRAISE FAMOUS MEN *1941*
James Agee/Walker Evans

In Céline the surrealism of the old world, and in Agee the realism of the new world, accepted modes of expression were inadequate to the subject. Agee welcomes the collaboration of the camera to make visible what defies description. The photographs of Walker Evans, the revelations of Agee's prose, constitute an American testament of faith, a portrait of life that is transcendent. This book defies imitation but its example continues to make converts. It would appear that only Americans convert the new into trash, into junk, yet feel the presence of life in worn-out objects, made holy by use. It is common for the backward and the rural folk to feel it, and it may have its origin in the pioneer experience of starting from scratch, in the consecration of an object through use, through survival. This sentiment is further nourished by frugality, by identifying the object with the task, both emblematic of life. In Agee, the burden of this intent is religious, and on occasion almost unbearably poignant.

Meanwhile the floor, the roof, the opposed walls, the furniture, in their hot gloom: all watch upon one hollow center. The intricate tissue is motionless. The swan, the hidden needle, hold their course. On the red-gold wall sleeps a long, faded, ellipsoid smear of light. The vase is dark. Upon the leisures of the earth the whole home is lifted before the approach of darkness as a boat and as a sacrament.

A book of Scripture, illustrated with its own articles of faith.

THE WIFE OF MARTIN GUERRE *1941*
Janet Lewis

Here is a novel that is short, free of violence and sex, life-enhancing, profound, and told as simply as an old wives' tale. Based on the records of a trial held in the sixteenth century, it concerns Bertrande de Rols, the wife of Martin Guerre, whose husband one day walked out of her life. Years later one claiming to be this man returns and takes his former place at her side. They are alike in appearance, but in Bertrande de Rols a kernel of suspicion begins to torment her. She loves this man, but she feels certain he is not the one she married. The problems that arise torment and confound her, as they challenge and confound the reader. Janet Lewis proves to be the perfect medium to transcribe this experience from one age to another, startling the reader with the relevance of "old-fashioned" truths.

A torment that is cleansing—*poi s'ascose nel foco che gli affina*—is one of the soul's admitted hungers in the light of its burden of guilt. To be human is to feel it, and to cease to feel it is to be either less or more than human, and one of the novelties of our age is that such extremes are not unusual.

169

Until we *know* what it is to be human, being human will naturally elude many people persuaded they both have, and prefer, other options. In her simple and complex humanity, the wife of Martin Guerre provides a touchstone for what is human, and many readers will experience the nature of her torment with a sense of discovery and release.

UNDER THE VOLCANO *1947*
Malcolm Lowry

Against the drift of the times, and the author's intent, this
is both a modern and romantic novel. It is the nearest to
the novel Fitzgerald should have written, at once tender and
brutal in its portrayal of a crack-up. Lowry manages to
salvage from a shattered life a full spectrum of the alcoholic's split vision. A friendly demon may have whispered
to the author that the proper setting for this drama would be
in Mexico, where the landscape lends itself to hallucination.
Until a better one comes along, it is the gringo's novel of life
south of the border. Lowry knows its color, its mescal flavor,
its matchless blending of the past and the present into something vividly remembered. Both the appeal and the terror—
for the hallucinating exile—of the intense light and shade,
the serene mornings, the drugged siestas, the crumbling of
composure with a crack of thunder and the magnesium flare
of lightning, dissolving the night. A country of malevolent
contrasts, made to order for the alcoholic of genius. Mexico
collaborates. At the time Lowry was there, in the late thirties,
Cuernavaca offered the ideal commingling of all elements,

old, new, and recently imported. The key inspiration proved to be that of casting the protagonist as the Consul. This provided Lowry with precisely the distance he seemed to need for his affectionate, inspired, and brutally candid portrait of his condemned life.

THE FALL *1956*
Albert Camus

The two great passions of Camus's creative life—his metaphysical craving for clarity and truth, his sympathy with all those who suffer injustice—are dramatized in *The Stranger*. On occasion the metaphysics fault the fiction, as they do here. The same concerns are at the heart of *The Fall,* but the author's intent is more complicated, even deliberately ambiguous. Who has fallen? The first-person narration of J. Baptiste Clamence presumes to be the confession of a Parisian lawyer famous for his defense of widows and orphans. The mockery is explicit. It is soon apparent that Clamence bears an echoing resemblance to the author, who has been at pains to inform the reader, in an epigraph, that Clamence is "A Hero of Our Time," an aggregate of our vices rather than a particular individual. This disclaimer seems too obvious. That Camus is doing more than confess Clamence gives *The Fall* the resonant ambiguity that peculiarly excites the modern reader. Nor is it all merely an artful tour de force, where brilliance of performance outweighs the usual considerations. In comprehending Clamence, in fathoming his guilt, the reader feels that Camus has found the ideal occasion for his own revelations. The fascination and achievement of this short novel lie in this overlapping portrait, in which reader, author, and Clamence mutually confront a disturbing likeness.

I'M NOT STILLER *1958*
Max Frisch

The qualities that distinguish great European fiction—
perception, a ranging mind, assured craft—are present in
this novel by a Swiss writer. I have chosen it because so few
American readers have read it, but many of those who have
admire it as much as I do. In his tone and point of view
Frisch recalls Thomas Mann, even to setting one scene in a
sanatorium at Davos. He uses, rather than abuses, this
parallel, in a manner that Mann would have appreciated.
The drama of Stiller is that of a man who refuses to accept
his own past—a fresh twist on the identity crisis—but as I
reread the novel this central conflict becomes of secondary
interest. Frisch is a marvelous writer, and his portraits of
women seem to me among the best of modern fiction.

At that time Julika had a dog, a fox terrier, of the sort
that goes with childless couples. He was called Foxie or, in
the language of this country—which, by the way, is an
extremely pleasant language, not exactly melodious perhaps, but down-to-earth and, when you listen to it closely,
not unmusical—Foxli. She loved him, naturally, otherwise
they needn't have had him at all; that's the nice thing

about dogs, you either love them or you needn't have them. Stiller could never understand how anyone could love Foxli, and he was scarcely able to read the message in Foxli's eyes. . . . He referred to the dog sarcastically as the Sacred Beast.

Frisch's affectionate irony makes a poignant story out of the tragic mismatch of Stiller and Frau Julika, a love affair so doomed it can be borne only through Julika's report on the matter. Stiller's crisis of soul will be new to readers who have assumed matters of religious doctrine are no longer urgent since they are largely absent from the American novel.

A HALL OF MIRRORS *1967*
Robert Stone

Among younger writers, I like the way Robert Stone is both traditional and innovative. He has read the good books, he has led the hard life, and he brings to the novel a vision of life that begins where black humor ends. Stone looks steadily, perhaps obsessively, at the human abuse and waste explicitly made in U.S.A. He has no tricks. Like Céline he reports what seems obvious. In my judgment, we must go back to Céline to find writing so seamlessly welded to nightmare, a first harrowing voyage to the neon-lit American night. We have need of such a writer, and perhaps writers will ensure that he gets a reading. Narrative drive and unforced lyrical power come as readily to Stone as this first panel in his view of hell. He seems to me one of the first to write out of this experience, rather than to brilliantly write about it, holding the reader in a light that is incandescent, but without heat. The burden Stone was able to bear in writing this novel is one that his gifts impose on the reader, a hellish landscape of No Exits, on the American plan.

ONE HUNDRED YEARS OF SOLITUDE *1970*
Gabriel García Márquez

I have reserved this book to the last so that the reader might judge two things for himself—the variations and achievements of the true-to-life mode; the limitations it imposes on the imagination. Of the writers on this list only García Márquez might have said to himself, "Just imagine!" as he sat down to write. *One Hundred Years of Solitude* is his attempt to be true to the imagination. It is not an accessory to the world of facts, but a maker of facts, the prime mover.

It is García Márquez's intent, as it was that of Cervantes, whose spirit haunts this chronicle, to record in the history of one family the tragicomedy of human existence. Macondo, a mythical town, has its rise and its fall in these one hundred years. The reader shaped by verifiable, true-to-life fiction inhabited by characters almost as real as his neighbors will find the swirling world of Macondo a strain until he has adapted to its tempests. There is no way for the true-to-life mode of fiction to comprehend the tumult of García Márquez's vision. No way. It had to be imagined, and the gist of it captured in a style adequate to its immense disorder.

178

"I am certain of nothing but the holiness of the Heart's affections," said Keats, "and the truth of Imagination." So is García Márquez. *One Hundred Years of Solitude* has the virtue of putting first things first.

If Fiction Is So Smart,
Why Are We So Stupid?

I sometimes marvel why the world is not a better place, and most of us are not better people, having read the great books, seen the great paintings, and shared the elevation of great music. Why are we, who presume to be so eager, so little affected by the works of art? Why do words of insight and thoughts that exalt us so easily enter one opening and go out another, leaving small trace? Why does the higher consciousness created by the artist make so little impression on the social conscience, man's concern and affection for his fellow men? No answer exists beyond the fact that man's higher faculties are slow to modify his lower, and in that sliver of light we call historical time he makes wars, he makes news, but he makes small progress. The devil, too, is a reader, and reads to cultivate his talent for devilment.

If all readers could read one good novel only, and read it as our forefathers once read the Bible, if that one book were read and not erased by another, if it were part of both our higher and our lower natures, the craft of fiction might exert on us all a perceptible influence for the better. We have made so much of the private experience, the common experience is the one we distrust. In the absence of shared experience we futilely pursue happiness.

> What ails me is the absolute frustration of my primeval societal instinct. The hero illusion starts with the individualist illusion, and all resistances ensue. I think societal instinct much deeper than sex instinct—and societal repression much more devastating. There is no repression of the sexual individual comparable to the repression of the societal man in me, by the individual ego, my own and everybody else's. I am weary even of my own individuality, and simply nauseated by other people's.

This from a letter of D. H. Lawrence's. It has been left to fiction to report on this ad nauseam, and a profound distaste for the ego trip turns many readers away from the novel.

How restore to the difficult craft of fiction, based on individual effort and experience, the pleasures of a common and shared experience rather than one based on distinctions? How, when the distinctions are what we strive to share?

Lawrence had no answer, but he knew what ailed him. We have no answer but we are ignorant of what ails us.

It is tiresomely said that we have lost our way. We have never lost our way. We have followed our way to its predictable conclusions, its numberless dead ends. Our pursuit of novelty now takes us into space, having depleted the surprises of this planet. Taking off, after all, is our special talent: destinations have invariably been a letdown. We are, indeed, cunning and inscrutable creatures, mad for facts that we must turn into fiction to possess. If it's about man, it's about fiction, and the better the fiction, the more it's about. The worse the fiction, the less we all have of the facts of life. If we are to be more rather than less human—one of our many stimulating options—we will turn from what we see around us, and attend to the promptings within us. The imagination made us human, but *being* human, becoming more human, is a greater burden than we imagined. We have no choice but to imagine ourselves more human than we are.

75 76 77 10 9 8 7 6 5 4 3 2 1